Treating Stress and Anxiety

A Practitioner's Guide to Evidence-based Approaches

Dr Lillian Nejad
Katerina Volny

Crown House Publishing Limited
www.crownhouse.co.uk
www.chpus.com

First published by

Crown House Publishing Ltd
Crown Buildings, Bancyfelin, Carmarthen, Wales, SA33 5ND, UK
www.crownhouse.co.uk

and

Crown House Publishing Company LLC
6 Trowbridge Drive, Suite 5, Bethel, CT 06801-2858, USA
www.CHPUS.com

British Library Cataloguing-in-Publication Data
A catalogue entry for this book is available
from the British Library.

ISBN 978-184590077-9

LCCN 2007932740

Printed and bound in the USA

Contents

List of figures

List of tables

Acknowledgements

We would like to thank all our colleagues, supervisors, and friends who provided much encouragement and support as we were writing this book.

A special thanks to our colleagues who took the time to review the book: Dr Cindy Williams, Dr Robert Kruk, Dr Robyn Gallucci, and Elizabeth Sommerville—your comments and suggestions were greatly appreciated. We thank our families and especially acknowledge our partners, Brian and George, for their contributions to this project, particularly in the development and marketing of the Relaxation CD in the early days, and their unwavering belief in us and what we have to offer. It is also important to thank our former and current professors, lecturers, supervisors, and clients for enriching us with your knowledge, passion, and expertise, without which this book would not be possible. And finally, thank you to David Bowman, Karen Bowman, Mark Tracten, and everyone else at Crown House Publishing for seeing the value in this endeavour and helping it come to fruition.

Foreword

As a clinical psychologist who has taught counselling skills and cognitive behaviour therapy approaches at masters and doctoral levels for over 20 years, I have witnessed important developments in the field during that time. One of the most exciting has been the emergence of high-quality therapy handbooks for practitioners and clients which are simultaneously evidence-based and user-friendly. This type of text includes explanations for the practitioner which refer to research findings, as well as assessment and practice guidelines. The most user-friendly handbooks include a full range of handouts and worksheets for clients written in lay language, and a companion CD so that the handouts can be readily reproduced by simply printing them out.

Treating Stress and Anxiety: A Practitioner's Guide to Evidence-Based Approaches fulfils all my criteria for an excellent practical and user-friendly clinician's handbook. It contains a wide range of explanations, activities, and resources for use with clients presenting with stress and anxiety difficulties, and covers the major evidence-based approaches, ranging from cognitive restructuring and progressive exposure, to mindfulness. In addition, since anxiety disorders commonly co-occur with other issues such as depression, anger, substance use, communication problems, and self-acceptance difficulties, the handbook also offers explanations and strategies for dealing with these and other related problems. I was pleased to see sections on how to address more general life-style issues such as thoroughly assessing and then improving exercise, sleep, eating patterns, health behaviours, pleasant activities and time management. The book also includes concepts and resources based on the stages of change and motivation enhancement literature These are increasingly recognised as crucial in initial stages of therapy for many individuals.

I expect this text to be invaluable for experienced therapists and beginners alike. For novice therapists and early career practitioners, this handbook makes clear the basis of approaches that can be taken to managing anxiety and stress, and what a full therapeutic package will look like. The guide provides a starting point and resources which would otherwise be very time consuming to construct from scratch. By having explanatory handouts for clients available, novice therapists can also find out how to translate the technical clinical information they are learning into language and examples that a client can relate to.

More experienced therapists are generally aware of the need to develop a library of books and resources to use with different clients in specific contexts. In particular, since most of the therapeutic 'work' is done between sessions, having access to this guide's explanatory materials for clients to read at home, and a range of assessment and home activities, will make the process much more efficient for both the therapist and the client.

After the thorough guidelines and resources on therapeutic assessment and intervention strategies, the handbook explores how to work with the later stages of therapy. Because making positive changes can sometimes be easier than *maintaining* the changes once a client finishes therapy, the handbook addresses how to prevent relapse, and how to think about and work with lapses to ensure that the client's gains are maintained over time.

The language a therapist uses is extremely important because the way techniques, concepts and approaches are described can either help clients to understand and accept new ideas or create resistance. Similarly, the sorts of examples that are offered can make concepts concrete and help clients to relate to them, or they can be abstract and foreign sounding. The language in this guidebook is thought out very carefully – for example, explanatory handouts often include normalising statements so the client does not feel 'odd' or labeled, and strategies are approached from the point of view of being potentially useful suggestions rather than methods to fix a 'pathology' or 'disorder'.

In many contexts group therapy is a potentially cost-effective (for client and therapist) and powerful way to assist individuals to deal with anxiety and stress. Group therapy has the advantage of helping clients meet others who have similar issues, so that they feel less alone, are able to normalise their experience, and to be supported by a range of people. Furthermore, when anxieties involve social fears, a client can gain enormously from taking the risk of disclosing feelings and concerns to others, and from being supported by peers when they do so. Most practitioner handbooks do not give specific guidelines for how to apply the relevant strategies and approaches in a group therapy context. The presence in *Treating Stress and Anxiety* of a detailed chapter on how to apply the ideas to group work adds to the broad practical use of the text. Topics covered include how to address client fears about joining a group, useful group structure and agreements, what an eight-week group program might look like, and even an evaluation form for clients to complete at the end.

I see two additional strengths of *Treating Stress and Anxiety,* and they are the CD-ROMs that supplement the handbook. First, the handbook comes with a CD-ROM so that client handouts can be printed out. And second, there is a companion CD—*Relaxation Techniques: Reduce Stress & Anxiety and Enhance Well-Being* (available separately) that offers a variety of guided relaxation exercises. An important component of dealing with anxiety or stress problems is being able to assist individuals acquire better relaxation skills. Relaxation CDs can be a core part of this process. Whilst there are a host of relaxation CDs available in the community, I have found that most of them are not really suitable for clients who come to a Psychology Clinic. Most commonly available CDs are 'new age' in style, and although these can be appropriate for some clients, they often are not consistent with the evidence-based practice approach that infuses how allied health professionals are increasingly choosing (and encouraged) to practice. The companion *Relaxation Techniques* CD includes a range of relaxation approaches from progressive muscle relaxation to guided imagery and affirmation-style approaches. The CD also facilitates the learning process for clients by including separate tracks that introduce the skill of relaxation, that present guidelines for practising the techniques, and that explain the rationale for each of the seven exercises.

I congratulate Lillian Nejad and Katerina Volny for compiling such a comprehensive and practical resource. While the title promises that the text offers a guide to working with anxiety and stress difficulties, the handouts and materials are in reality much more broadly applicable to a wide variety of client problem areas. I hope that practitioners, educators, and student therapists include this text in their own library ... and refer to it often.

Eleanor H. Wertheim, PhD, FAPS
Professor (Personal Chair)
School of Psychological Science
La Trobe University
Bundoora (Melbourne), Victoria, Australia

Co-author of *Skills for Resolving Conflict* and *I Win, You Win*

Wertheim, E. H., Love, A., Peck, C., & Littlefield, L. (2006). *Skills for resolving conflict: A co-operative problem solving approach (2nd edn)*. Melbourne, Victoria: Eruditions.

Wertheim, E.H., Love, A., Littlefield, L., & Peck, C. (1992). *I win: You win*. Melbourne: Penguin Pub.

Introduction

This workbook and supplementary CD provide clinicians and therapists with a practical guide to evidence-based techniques that help reduce stress and anxiety as well as enhance quality of life. The techniques discussed are aimed at adults. This book endeavours to help clinicians deliver best practice treatments to individuals and groups who present with anxiety and stress-related issues as well as those who would generally benefit from building their emotional resilience. The purpose of the practical skills within this manual is to minimise distress and maximise efficacy in many areas of living, and to impart skills to live life in a happier and healthier manner. We hope that the reader also finds the skills presented in this book to be valuable for enhancing their clients' quality of life. Much like a healthy diet helps improve and maintain physical health and prevent disease, developing skills that manage stress and anxiety can be viewed as essential in enhancing and maintaining emotional health and preventing mental health problems.

Evidence-based treatment is increasingly in demand from a range of services, often linked to the funding of these services, and therefore, it is an important aspect of service provision. Current evidence-based guidelines recommend cognitive behavioural therapy as the primary treatment for persons experiencing anxiety disorders; therefore, this manual provides a practical guide and resources focused primarily on cognitive behavioural techniques for both individual therapy and group programmes. This text also provides guidelines for assessing the match between the client and therapist, and reviewing the progress of therapy, so that when appropriate, clients with difficulties outside the scope of expertise of the therapist can be referred elsewhere.

This text is a clinician's guide and should be useful to a variety of professionals (psychologists, psychiatrists, medical practitioners, mental health workers, social workers) who espouse diverse theoretical perspectives such as cognitive behavioural therapy, medical/biological models, biopsychosocial models, psychodynamic perspectives, neurolinguistic programming, narrative therapy, family therapy, and interpersonal therapy. The workbook is written in straightforward, uncomplicated language to enable practitioners to impart the information and skills to their clients easily and effectively. The presentation of this information is not intended to replace a broad range of existing practices, but is designed to be accessible to a wide audience, and complement current practices.

The chapters and exercises are provided in a format that is easy to use and includes handouts and worksheets for clients. The first three chapters focus on providing an overview of anxiety and stress by presenting the symptoms, discussing how to conduct a thorough assessment, and describing the treatment guidelines according to the latest research. Chapters 4 to 8 introduce the various strategies and techniques to treat anxiety and stress. Chapter 9 discusses co-morbid issues including depression, substance use, self-concept and identity, anger, and communication difficulties. Two group programmes, *Reducing and Managing Anxiety and Panic* and *Enhancing Well-Being and Reducing Stress* are outlined in Chapter 10. This guide also includes comprehensive resources for practitioners to offer to clients including psychoeducation handouts and skills development worksheets. The handouts and worksheets are located at the end of each chapter arranged in the order they are introduced in the text and are easily accessible on the supplementary CD to photocopy for clients.

A CD of relaxation exercises, *Relaxation Techniques: Reduce Stress and Anxiety and Enhance Well-Being*, is also available to complement this text (ISBN: 978-1845900786). The CD provides relaxation techniques that have been demonstrated to be effective in research studies and clinical practice. An introduction to relaxation, guidelines for relaxation, and a clear rationale for each technique are in audio format on separate tracks on the CD. There are a wide range of techniques to suit a variety of individual preferences. The voice of the practitioner and the background music are soothing, and do not distract from the relaxation task. The CD can be used as a standalone therapy tool to assist clients to practise skills between therapy sessions or in conjunction with other techniques like graded exposure. Feedback about this CD from both practitioners (clinical psychologists, psychiatrists, general medical practitioners, mental health nurses, and social workers) and clients alike has been overwhelmingly positive.

The simple and straightforward manner in which this material is presented in both the workbook and CD is the kind of approach that we have found works best for a wide range of clients.

- This text comprises a clinician's manual with structured worksheets and handouts for the management of stress and anxiety and the treatment of anxiety disorders.
- This manual is designed in accordance with evidence-based treatment and extensive clinical experience.

Chapter 1

A brief overview of anxiety and stress

Experiencing anxiety and stress are normal parts of everyday life. There is probably not a day that goes by that we don't hear someone say, "I am so stressed ..." Stress and anxiety-related problems are likely to increase over time as the world continues to move at a faster pace, as we become more overwhelmed by our infinite access to information, as our expectations rise to achieve success quickly and easily, and as we continue to place an inordinate focus on financial success and beauty. Of course, stress and anxiety have a positive impact on our lives as well. They serve to stimulate, motivate, and challenge us, and they serve as warnings and activate our bodies to react accordingly. Therefore, we can view both stress and anxiety along a continuum, acknowledging that not enough stress or arousal and too much, too intense, or prolonged stress and arousal, lead to poor functioning and impairment, while some stress is necessary to lead a fulfilling life. This is well demonstrated by the Yerkes-Dodson arousal and performance curve, shown below.

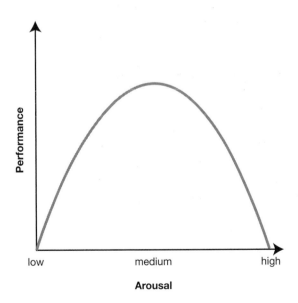

Figure 1: Yerkes-Dodson diagram (Yerkes & Dodson, 1908)

Given the useful functions of stress and anxiety, the goal of therapy is never to eliminate these states entirely, but to identify the ways in which they have a negative impact and to learn ways of managing stress and anxiety more effectively in these situations and in general. A brief overview of stress and anxiety disorders is discussed below followed by prevalence rates and relevant co-morbid issues.

Stress

Stress is sometimes difficult to differentiate from anxiety, as these terms are often used interchangeably. However, stress is defined here as a state of tension that occurs when there are too many demands in the environment, or when we experience or anticipate experiencing a situation that is perceived as threatening, unpleasant, or unfamiliar. Examples of such demands and situational triggers include being overloaded with work, having difficulties in relationships, moving to another city, being asked to make a speech, being under financial strain, and taking care of children without adequate support. There are also factors that make us more vulnerable to stress including poor eating and sleeping patterns, excessive drug use, lack of exercise, social isolation, physical illness, and lack of regular involvement in enjoyable and relaxing activities. The experience of stress has a variety of physical, cognitive, emotional, and behavioural effects, not totally dissimilar to the effects of anxiety. Handout 1.1 provides an explanation of stress for clients including common triggers and ways to manage stress. Handout 1.2 displays the many effects of stress.

Anxiety disorders

Anxiety is an emotion that prompts a physical response that allows us to react quickly to a real or perceived threat. This response is called the "fight or flight" mechanism. When the anxiety response is too intense or prolonged, or if someone experiences repeated actual or perceived threats to their or their significant others' lives, it can lead to anxiety disorders. Among American adults, there is a lifetime prevalence for anxiety disorders of approximately 29% (Kessler et al., 2005) and 18% have an anxiety disorder within a 12-month period (Kessler et al., 2005) (see Table 1).

The Diagnostic and Statistical Manual of Psychiatric Disorders (4th edn) (DSM-IV-TR: APA, 2000) is a widely used text that presents detailed descriptions and diagnostic criteria for anxiety disorders. The following is only a brief overview of anxiety disorders. It is recommended that you obtain a DSM-IV-TR to refer to when making or understanding a diagnosis. When considering the diagnosis of an anxiety disorder, it is necessary to ascertain whether the symptoms are better accounted for by the effects of a substance, a general medical

Table 1: Lifetime and one-year prevalence rates of anxiety disorders according to National Comorbidity Study Replication (NCS-R) (Kessler et al., 2005; Kessler, Chiu, Demler & Walters, 2005)*

Anxiety disorders	Lifetime prevalence (%)	One-year prevalence (%)
Generalised anxiety disorder (GAD)	5.7	3.1
Panic disorder (with or without agoraphobia)	4.7	2.7
Agoraphobia without panic	1.4	0.8
Post-traumatic stress disorder (PTSD)	6.8	3.5
Obsessive compulsive disorder (OCD)	1.6	1.0
Specific phobia	12.5	8.7
Social phobia (social anxiety disorder)	12.1	6.8

*NCS-R study based on sample from the United States. Refer to the WHO World Mental Health Surveys for prevalence rates for Colombia, Mexico, Belgium, France, Germany, Italy, Netherlands, Spain, Ukraine, Lebanon, Nigeria, Japan, and the People's Republic of China (Demyttenaere et al., 2004). Prevalence rates for the UK can be found in Singleton et al., (2001) and rates for Australia can be found in the Australian National Survey of Mental Health and Well-Being (NSMHWB) (Australian Bureau of Statistics, 1997). Keep in mind that national prevalence rates vary, at least in part, due to difference in measures and criteria used in studies and variations in response rates.

condition, or another mental disorder. In some instances, an individual may meet the diagnostic criteria for more than one anxiety disorder. Furthermore, co-morbidity with other disorders such as depression or substance abuse disorders is common. Also, keep in mind that it is only when anxiety is having a significant impact on a person's ability to carry on with their usual activities and responsibilities, such as employment, relationships, and recreational pursuits, that it is considered to be at the level of a disorder. Anxiety that is a problem but does not interfere with usual routines and activities may be termed "sub-clinical anxiety". Diagnoses should be confirmed by a trained mental health clinician.

A summary of the distinguishing characteristics of anxiety disorders is provided below. Handout 1.3 and 1.4 describe the fight and flight response, the cycle of anxiety, and the common effects of anxiety for clients.

Generalised anxiety disorder (GAD)

GAD connotes the experience of persistent and excessive anxiety and worry about a variety of potential things, events, and situations on more days than not for a period of six months, with at least three symptoms of the following: restlessness, easily fatigued, difficulty concentrating, irritability, muscle tension, and disturbed sleep. The intensity, duration, or frequency of the anxiety is out of proportion with the usual impact of events affecting the person at that time. The lifetime prevalence of GAD is 5.7% and 3.1% experience GAD within a twelve-month period (Kessler et al., 2005; Kessler, Chiu, Demler & Walters, 2005) (see Table 1). Note that if the excessive worry is only in relation to illness, health-related problems, and/or potential injury then the diagnosis is not GAD but hypochondriasis, or possibly obsessive compulsive disorder.

Panic disorder (with or without agoraphobia)

Panic disorder is defined as the presence of at least two recurrent, unexpected panic attacks followed by at least one month of persistent concern about having another panic attack, worry about the possible implications or consequences of panic attacks, or significant behavioural change related to the panic attacks.

Panic attacks are described as a period of sudden onset of intense apprehension, fearfulness, or terror, and often feelings of impending doom that manifest in a number of physical symptoms including shortness of breath, heart palpitations or accelerated heart rate, chest pain or discomfort, feeling dizzy or faint, choking or smothering sensations, chills or hot flushes, and trembling or shaking. The intense physical sensations are usually interpreted as signs of having a heart attack or of "going crazy" and therefore people often think they are going to die or lose control.

Panic disorder may occur with or without agoraphobia, and agoraphobia may occur on its own. Agoraphobia is described as the fear of being in or going to places or situations from which escape might be difficult or embarrassing, or in which help may not be available in the event of having panic-like symptoms, leading to avoidance of these situations. In the United States, although about 23% of American adults have experienced panic attacks, the lifetime prevalence for panic disorder without agoraphobia is 3.7% and 1.1% for panic disorder with agoraphobia (Kessler et al., 2006). Those with agoraphobia are more likely to have co-morbid diagnoses (Kessler et al., 2006).

Post-traumatic stress disorder (PTSD)

Post-traumatic stress disorder can occur when a person is confronted with a situation of actual, perceived, or threatened death or serious injury to themself or others, where they have responded with intense fear, helplessness, or horror. The symptoms include a variety of intrusive memories of the event, avoidance behaviours, dissociative responses, and hypervigilance for a period of more than one month. The lifetime prevalence of PTSD among American adults is approximately 6.8%, and the twelve-month prevalence is between 3.5% (Kessler et al., 2005; Kessler, Chiu, Demler & Walters, 2005). People with PTSD often have co-morbid issues including depression, substance abuse, sleep disorders, and chronic pain.

Acute stress disorder

Acute stress disorder occurs as a result of the same circumstances as PTSD; however, it is diagnosed when the duration of symptoms is more than two days and less than four weeks.

Obsessive compulsive disorder (OCD)

OCD is characterised by persistent and intrusive thoughts (obsessions) that cause substantial anxiety and distress, which are managed by ritualistic and time-consuming behaviours (compulsions) that temporarily relieve the distress. A common example is the persistent thought that some kind of harmful germs may be present, leading to an excessive and problematic amount of cleaning and handwashing to decrease the anxiety and worry. Other compulsive behaviours include checking (if the door is locked, the iron is off), repeating rituals (tapping a table a certain number of times before eating), organising behaviours (making sure clothes, CDs, food items are ordered in a certain way), and hoarding (saving all newspapers). People who have OCD are aware that their thoughts and behaviours are irrational but are unable to tolerate the anxiety that accompanies their obsessions.

Specific phobia

The anxiety disorder with the highest lifetime prevalence is specific phobia. When substantial anxiety is provoked by a specific feared object or situation, it is termed a specific phobia. Common specific phobias include a fear of spiders, closed spaces, and flying. The most prevalent specific phobia among women is a fear of animals and among men it is the fear of heights (Curtis et al., 1998). Again, it is not considered a disorder if it does not interfere significantly with a person's functioning.

Social phobia (social anxiety disorder)

Social phobia is the third most common psychiatric disorder with a lifetime prevalence of 12.1% and a twelve-month prevalence of 6.8% (Kessler et al., 2005; Kessler, Chiu, Demler & Walters, 2005). Individuals with social phobia do not necessarily lack social skills, rather they fear being negatively evaluated or judged by others in social situations. They usually fear being embarrassed or looking foolish and dislike being the centre of attention. As in cases of specific phobia, people with social phobia avoid the feared situation, e.g., parties, work functions, classrooms. About a third of people with lifetime social anxiety disorder only experience anxiety in relation to speaking fears, e.g., public speaking, however, the majority generalise their fear to the majority of inter-personal situations (Kessler, Stein & Berglund, 1998). People who have a social phobia, particularly those who are anxious in a variety of situations, often present with co-morbid issues including depression, substance use/abuse, and other anxiety disorders.

Co-morbid disorders

A significant proportion of individuals who have an anxiety disorder have co-morbid psychiatric disorders, mainly another anxiety disorder, a depressive disorder, or a substance abuse disorder (Brown & Barlow, 1992; Cox, Norton, Swinson & Endler, 1990; Kessler, Chui, Demler & Walters, 2005; Kushner, Sher & Beitman, 1990; Lecrubier, 1998; Litz, Penk, Gerardi & Keane, 1992; Sanderson, DiNardo, Rapee & Barlow, 1990; Schneier et al., 1992; Steketee, 1993). Co-morbid depression and substance abuse are briefly discussed below.

Anxiety and depression

Research indicates that anxiety disorders usually precede depressive disorders by up to eleven years (Kessler et al., 2005; van Ameringen, Mancini, Styan & Donison, 1991) so it is no surprise that anxiety and depression can often present concurrently. While this manual focuses on the management and treatment of stress and anxiety, some of the cognitive behavioural techniques described in this book are relevant to those who have a primary diagnosis of depression (particularly Chapters 4, 5 and 6). There is some evidence that treatment for one disorder can lead to improvements in co-morbid conditions. Brown, Antony & Barlow (1995) found that patients with panic disorder who underwent cognitive behavioural therapy experienced a decrease in co-morbid conditions.

Distinguishing between depressive and anxiety symptoms is important when considering the primary disorder to be treated. See Table 2 to compare anxiety and depressive symptoms. Although research indicates that anxiety disorders generally predate mood disorders, it is useful to verify this by reviewing the history of the emergence of symptoms to determine the primary diagnosis. For instance, avoidance of previously enjoyable activities due to anxiety is likely to make a person more vulnerable to depression. Likewise, a period of lowered mood and activity that occurs with depression may lead a person to be apprehensive and anxious when trying to recommence activities. A comprehensive assessment of sleeping patterns can also elucidate whether anxiety or depression is more prominent. For example, difficulty falling asleep due to persistent worrying may denote a primary anxiety issue, whereas early morning waking is a common symptom of depression.

Table 2: Symptoms of depression and anxiety

Depression	Anxiety
• Lowered mood	• Panic attacks involving increased heart and breathing rate, chest pains, feeling hot and dizzy, or nausea
• Loss of interest in pleasurable activities	
• Low motivation	• Avoidance behaviours
• Low energy	• Difficulty falling asleep
• Fatigue	• Difficulty concentrating
• Psychomotor retardation or restlessness	• Irritability
• Appetite, weight changes	• Easily startled, hypervigilant
• Disturbed sleeping patterns	• Excessive worrying
• Poor concentration, memory problems	• Feelings of fear, anxiety, stress
• Feelings of guilt, shame, hopelessness	• Cognitions related to fear of judgement, not being able to cope or escape
• Cognitions about being worthless, helpless	
• Suicidal thoughts and behaviour	

Source: DSM-IV-TR (2000)

For a primary depressive disorder you will need to refer to a text that deals with depression (see recommended books in Appendix A); however, handouts related to depression can be found in Chapter 9 of this book.

Anxiety and substance use/abuse

Up to 15% of individuals who present with an anxiety disorder also have a substance use disorder (twelve-month prevalence rate, Grant et al., 2004). People use and abuse substances for a variety of reasons including managing symptoms associated with stress and anxiety; however, it can also serve to maintain and worsen these problems in the long term. It is important to assess clients' current substance use patterns particularly in relation to how this may interfere with therapy, e.g., attendance, motivation, exposure work. A medical assessment and management of detoxification and withdrawal may be required. Chapter 9 provides information on examining when substance use may be a problem that needs to be addressed.

What is stress?

Stress is a state of tension that occurs when there are too many demands in the environment or when we experience or anticipate experiencing a situation that is perceived as threatening, unpleasant, or unfamiliar. As well as having a physical effect on our body, stress can also affect our thoughts, feelings, and behaviours.

What triggers stress?

A wide variety of events or situations can trigger stress. These triggers can be both negative and positive in nature; for example, positive events like weddings, holidays, and promotions can trigger stress. Other examples of triggers are physical and mental health problems, relationship difficulties, being apart from family, deadlines for work, financial problems, being in crowds, public speaking, and simply too many things to do. There are also factors that make us more vulnerable to stress including poor eating and sleeping patterns, excessive drug use, lack of exercise, social isolation, physical illness, and lack of regular involvement in enjoyable and relaxing activities.

What happens when you get stressed?

Stress can trigger a variety of responses including physical reactions like tense muscles and headaches*, emotions like frustration and resentment, thoughts like, "I can't take this anymore," or "No one understands," and behaviours like not making time to eat, or snapping at others.

When does stress become a problem?

Not all stress is bad. People need a certain amount of stress to feel motivated to achieve goals and to face challenges in life. Stress that is too intense, too frequent, and/or long-lasting is unhealthy. (Too little stress can also be unhealthy but most of us don't suffer from that!) Prolonged stress can have a range of negative consequences both for your physical and your mental health as well as for your quality of life.

What can you do?

There are several things that you can do to reduce stress in your life. Helpful strategies include reacting differently to stressful situations, taking time to relax, leading a healthy lifestyle, and communicating your wants and needs to others. Managing your time effectively and having fun are also important. If stress is overwhelming and you don't know where to start, it may be useful to seek help from a professional, such as a psychologist or a counsellor, or to use a self-help book or CD as a guide.

---

* Consult with your GP if you experience persistent physical symptoms of stress to rule out any medical condition that may be contributing to or be the cause of these symptoms

Treating Stress and Anxiety © 2008 Crown House Publishing and Dr Lillian Nejad and Katerina Volny

The effects of stress

Listed below are some of the common effects of stress, including those reported by other people struggling with it. As you can see, stress can have many effects which can be divided into four categories: physical effects, effects to do with thinking, effects to do with feelings, and effects to do with behaviour (actions or non-actions).

Place a ✓ next to the ones you can relate to.

Physical	Thinking	Feeling	Behaviour
☐ Bad headaches	☐ I can't cope	☐ Stressed	☐ Staying in bed
☐ Pressure in head	☐ I am overloaded	☐ Frustrated	☐ Hyperactivity
☐ Increased heart rate	☐ I feel like crap	☐ Hopeless	☐ Nail-biting
☐ Sweating/hot flushes	☐ I can't change	☐ Self-pity	☐ Snapping at people
☐ Shaking	☐ How can I manage?	☐ Disappointed	☐ Scratching
☐ Diarrhoea/constipation	☐ Why me?	☐ On edge	☐ Difficulty sleeping
☐ No interest in sex	☐ I feel like a zombie	☐ Depressed	☐ Drinking alcohol
☐ Exhausted/tired	☐ I should be able to sort this out!	☐ Unhappy	☐ Not taking care of self
☐ Tight chest	☐ What's wrong?	☐ Hurt	☐ Avoiding other people
☐ Chest pains	☐ Can't they see that I'm busy!	☐ Angry	☐ Oversensitivity
☐ Weight gain/loss	☐ I don't have time!	☐ Desperate	☐ Losing temper easily
☐ Skin condition (e.g. rash)	☐ Here we go again	☐ Lonely	☐ Crying
☐ Feeling hot or cold	☐ I'm not going to be able to sleep	☐ Resentful	☐ Clenching jaw
☐ Health problems	☐ Nobody helps around here	☐ Vulnerable	☐ Pacing
☐ Pain (e.g. back pain)	☐ It's never going to end	☐ Insecure	☐ Impatient behaviour (in traffic, in a line, etc.)
☐ Menstrual cycle changes	☐ Do I have to do everything around here?	☐ Guilty	☐ Yelling at kids/partner
☐ Teeth grinding	☐ I can't do this, it's too much	☐ Panic	☐ Gambling
☐ Stomach pain or ulcer	☐ Don't want to talk to anyone	☐ Jealous	☐ Fidgeting
☐ Frequent colds	☐ Forgetfulness	☐ Ashamed	☐ Smoking more cigarettes
☐ Cramps or bloating	☐ Lack of concentration	☐ Numb	☐ Procrastinating
☐ Tension/tight muscles (e.g. neck, jaws)	☐ Confusion	☐ Shut down	☐ Overeating (junk food)
	☐ Constant worrying	☐ Moody	☐ Not making time to eat
		☐ Irritable	☐ Taking sick days
		☐ Grumpy	☐ Restlessness
		☐ Unmotivated	

9

What is anxiety?

Anxiety is not a bad emotion—it's a natural response that we all experience and it has a useful and protective function. Our bodies have an inbuilt mechanism called the "fight or flight" response that kicks in when we perceive a threat or are in danger. This is a physiological response that helps our bodies to prepare to either run away from danger or to physically fight and defend ourselves. A panic attack is a more intense and unpleasant experience of the fight or flight response. A panic attack is not life-threatening or an indication of a mental breakdown.*

So what actually happens in your body when you get anxious?

The flight or flight response causes the following changes to occur in your body:

1. Your brain receives information that there is a problem or threat, whether it is real or imagined.
2. Certain parts of your brain are activated in order to release chemicals and hormones that are needed to send messages to other parts of your body.
3. These chemicals cause your adrenal glands to release adrenaline.
4. Adrenaline causes you to become mentally very alert and it activates your senses.
5. Adrenaline increases your breathing rate, so that you take in more oxygen to enable you to run or fight.
6. Your heartbeat speeds up and your blood pressure increases.
7. Your liver releases sugar and other substances into the blood to supply quick energy to your muscles.
8. Sweating increases to help cool the body.
9. Blood is diverted to the muscles.

Now you're ready to either fight to defend yourself or to run away as fast you can.

When does anxiety become a problem?

Often it is inappropriate, not useful, or impossible to fight or run away in response to some of the real and imagined threats that you encounter. When this happens, your body is not able to release all the energy it has generated, it is not able to use all the oxygen you are inhaling, and it is not able to process the adrenaline. The short-term consequences of this are all the nasty effects of anxiety that you may be familiar with, such as dizziness, feeling nauseous, shaking, and scary or negative thoughts. Long-term effects of prolonged and intense anxiety include physical health problems and deterioration in your quality of life.

---

* It is recommended that you consult with your GP if you experience a panic attack to rule out any medical condition that may be contributing to or be the cause of anxiety symptoms.

It is common to respond to anxiety by avoiding situations that you think might make you anxious and by using or abusing substances to cope with your anxiety. Unfortunately, these strategies are counterproductive as they serve to increase your fear of situations and to add to your problems.

Cycle of anxiety

Anxiety is an emotional state associated with a series of changes in your body, and it can influence your thoughts, feelings, and behaviours. Your thoughts, feelings, and behaviours can, in turn, maintain the changes in your body, which then perpetuates the difficult thoughts and feelings, and before you know it you're caught in the vicious cycle of anxiety.

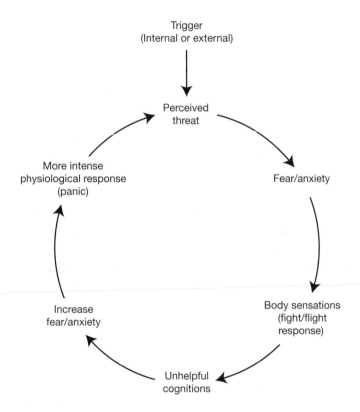

What can you do?

There are several techniques that interfere with the vicious cycle of anxiety. Helpful strategies include modifying your thinking patterns and relaxing your body. Anyone can learn these techniques. If you are experiencing severe or long-standing anxiety it is probably useful to seek help from a professional, such as a psychologist or a counsellor. Using self-help books or CDs that describe cognitive behavioural techniques for anxiety management can also be effective.

Treating Stress and Anxiety © 2008 Crown House Publishing and Dr Lillian Nejad and Katerina Volny

The effects of anxiety

Listed below are some of the common effects of anxiety as reported by other people struggling with this condition. As you can see, anxiety can have many effects, which can be divided into four categories: physical effects, effects to do with thinking, effects to do with feelings, and effects to do with behaviour (actions or non-actions).

Place a ✓ next to the ones you can relate to.

Physical	Thinking	Feeling	Behaviour
❑ Bad headaches	❑ I'm having a heart attack!	❑ Stressed	❑ Paralysed (not doing anything)
❑ Pressure in head	❑ I'm going to die!	❑ Afraid	❑ Avoid people
❑ Increased heart rate	❑ I'm having a nervous breakdown!	❑ Anxious	❑ Avoid going outside
❑ Palpitations	❑ I'm crazy!	❑ Frustrated	❑ Hyperactive
❑ Sweating/hot flushes	❑ I feel like shit	❑ Despair	❑ Restless
❑ Hyperventilating	❑ How can I manage?	❑ Hopeless	❑ Nail-biting
❑ Shaking	❑ I can't manage—why me?	❑ Self-pity	❑ Fidgeting
❑ Vomiting	❑ Why is this happening to me?	❑ Disappointed	❑ Difficulty sleeping
❑ Dry reaching	❑ I'm going mad	❑ On edge	❑ Substance abuse
❑ Diarrhoea/constipation	❑ I feel ridiculous—what am I scared	❑ Depressed	❑ Lack of self-care
❑ Exhausted/tired	of?	❑ Unhappy	❑ Oversensitive
❑ Tight chest	❑ I should be able to sort this out,	❑ Hurt	❑ Lose temper easily
❑ Chest pains	what's wrong?	❑ Angry	❑ Crying
❑ Sick/ill, nauseous	❑ Here we go again	❑ Desperate	❑ Jaw clenching
❑ Dizziness	❑ I'm not going to be able to sleep	❑ Lonely	❑ Pacing
❑ Tingling	❑ I'm not good enough	❑ Clingy	❑ Self-harm
❑ Weight gain/loss	❑ I'm going to be like this for the rest	❑ Vulnerable	❑ Impatient behaviour (e.g. in traffic
❑ Blotchy skin	of my life	❑ Insecure	or towards kids)
❑ Blushing	❑ Critical thoughts of self and/or	❑ Terrified	❑ Eat more/eat less
❑ Feeling hot or cold	others	❑ Panic	❑ Don't want to talk to anyone
❑ Dry mouth	❑ Memory loss	❑ Jealous	❑ Excessive handwashing
❑ Blurred vision	❑ Lack of concentration	❑ Ashamed	
❑ Jelly legs	❑ Paranoid thoughts	❑ Numb	
❑ Pain (e.g. back pain)		❑ Shut down	
❑ Psoriasis		❑ Mood swings	

Chapter 2

Identifying presenting problems and treatment goals

Enhancing wellness and working to prevent illnesses or disorders is the ultimate goal of most health practitioners. Unfortunately, by the time people visit a health professional, they are already experiencing significant difficulties. When was the last time you heard someone say, "I'm doing really well, can you help me stay that way?" Most of the time, we hear, "Something is really wrong and I want you to fix it." The good news is once people learn the techniques that help reduce current anxiety and stress, they can use them to help prevent future major difficulties, especially if practised regularly even when they are well. But if you do happen to see clients who aren't having major difficulties, consider introducing them to the techniques discussed in this workbook for preventative purposes as well as to enhance their well-being.

Understanding the client: the assessment

Understanding a client's issues is not always straightforward. Some clients present with one issue, like difficulty sleeping or chronic pain, but upon further assessment other problems related to their presenting issue are uncovered. Other clients may present with a variety of issues. For instance, a client may report having panic attacks, relationship difficulties, and a drinking problem. It may even be more vague than that: "Everything is hard! I'm not how I used to be." Sometimes it is difficult to know where to start.

Goals of the assessment phase

Generally, clinicians use the first few sessions of therapy to conduct a thorough assessment of all the presenting issues as well as relevant historical information—this is called the assessment phase. There are five main tasks in the initial stages of therapy, and particularly in the first session:

1. To introduce yourself and the content and process of therapy you provide e.g., your expertise and theoretical stance, length of sessions, frequency of sessions, length of treatment, confidentiality and limits of confidentiality;

2. To gain a reasonable understanding of the client's concerns in order to plan the goals of treatment;
3. To provide education about the client's concerns and about effective treatment;
4. To develop therapeutic rapport with the client; and
5. To foster realistic hope in the client.

Most people do not make it to a first session of therapy. This is due to a variety of reasons including lack of financial resources, it not being a priority, the stigma attached to obtaining psychological help, and not believing it is going to help. If clinicians spend one or more sessions only focusing on gathering information, some of it very personal or traumatic, a client may feel worse after the sessions and not be motivated to return. Therefore, as you are conducting your assessment, it is vital to spend some time during each session normalising their experience ("It can be difficult talking about personal things," or "People can feel drained after talking about their difficulties"); predicting their ambivalence ("A lot of people think that it's impossible to change, but I'd be out of a job if that were true," or "Sometimes people think that psychological treatment is not going to help, what do you think?"); and not only imparting the idea but demonstrating that change is possible ("Change is possible and learning certain skills will help you manage your anxiety better") by introducing and providing rationale for a brief behavioural technique like a breathing exercise, practising it during the session, and asking for feedback). Make sure you keep these other important goals in mind while you are conducting the assessment.

Discussing confidentiality

Before you conduct the assessment, it is paramount that you introduce the parameters of confidentiality in your therapeutic relationship with your clients. You should convey to your clients that what they discuss with you during your sessions will remain confidential but that there are some limits to confidentiality. They must be informed that you will be keeping records of the sessions, that these records will be securely stored, and who will be privy to the records (e.g., other staff members, your supervisor, the insurance company). Tell your clients with whom you will discuss their case and for what purpose (clinical review meetings, case conferences, research, supervision sessions, insurance reports).

They must be informed about the main exceptions to confidentiality and how these situations would be handled should they arise. The exceptions to confidentiality may vary slightly depending on where you practice; therefore, you should verify the ethical and legal boundaries within your own professional guidelines and federal and state laws. However, the general exceptions to confidentiality relate to protecting your client or others from harm should they reveal current suicidal risk, current abuse toward a child or an elder adult, and/or danger of violence to others, particularly if it is a specific person or persons. In addition, the client should be informed that if you are subpoenaed or given a court order, you must release information to a court of law. In addition to discussing these issues with your clients, it is helpful to have an information sheet outlining the details so that you can be assured that they have something to refer back to when necessary.

Conducting the assessment

The goal of an assessment is for the client and therapist to develop treatment goals that are realistic and have a good chance of success for the client. When multiple difficulties are present, the assessment will assist in prioritising difficulties so that the most important factors can become the focus of treatment. These goals are the foundation of the treatment that follows; they need to be relevant to the client, and developed in collaboration with the client, so that they have just as much commitment to addressing them as the therapist.

Sometimes the client will have a very clear idea about what is happening and why; however, a comprehensive assessment is still warranted as the client will benefit from an objective perspective on his or her problems. It can be helpful to inform the client that you will need to ask them several questions over one or more sessions to better understand their difficulties and to ascertain the best treatment or referral options.

An assessment generally involves asking questions to clarify the presenting problems and aspects of their history that elucidate the predisposing factors— the precipitating factors, the maintaining factors, and the protective factors— related to their presenting issue as well as their current coping mechanisms. An assessment tool for clinicians is provided in this chapter. The Emotional Health Check-up (Handout 4.1) in Chapter 4 is also a helpful assessment tool.

Assessment checklist

Presenting problems: Open questions—why presenting now?

Specific anxiety assessment: First time and most recent time this happened (when, where, symptoms, etc.). Triggers for anxiety (people, places, situations). What do you fear might happen? When the problem has been better or worse? When more likely to occur? What are the exceptions (when you would have expected anxiety or avoidance to occur but person was able to manage the symptoms/situation)? Factors that help you with this problem? Coping mechanisms? Avoidance behaviours?

Risk assessment: If suicidality, criminal behaviour, or violence present—history, intent, plan, means, protective factors.

Essential facts: Health and development in early childhood, relationship with parents and siblings, family environment (stable, secure, happy, or chaotic, traumatic), school and work history, drug use history, relationship history, traumas, accidents, grief and illnesses, history of family illness, mental illness or other problems, daily living skills, previous treatment.

Formulation: Vulnerabilities and stressors, presenting problems including risk, predisposing, precipitating, maintaining, protective factors, strengths and coping mechanisms, the individual's values, priorities, goals.

Handout 2.1 and the handouts in Chapter 1 provide education about psychological treatment and general information about stress and anxiety that clients can read in-between sessions. Assigning a self-monitoring task and practising a brief behavioural intervention like a short breathing exercise during the assessment phase is helpful in clarifying current problems as well as determining the client's ability and/or motivation to complete homework tasks and practise skills. Difficulties and barriers to completion of in-between session tasks can provide valuable information to improve your understanding of an individual's functioning, and this may sometimes reveal the need for a change in the treatment goals, nature of treatment strategies, or pace of treatment.

Clarifying the presenting problem

Pay particular attention to the impact of each issue on the client's functioning and how the different issues may be related to each other. For example, in the scenario with the client who presents with panic attacks and relationship and drinking problems, it would be important to clarify: How much is the client drinking (or using other substances)? Is this contributing to the relationship problems or did the relationship problems lead to increased drinking? How are the panic attacks affecting the relationship? Are panic attacks triggered by alcohol use or is alcohol a coping mechanism for anxiety? How often are the panic attacks and when did they start? How are these problems impairing daily functioning? Which of these problems is having the most significant impact on functioning? Validated measures of anxiety, depression, and functioning (e.g., Beck Depression Inventory (BDI), Y-BOCS, Beck Anxiety Disorder (BAI)) can be used to ascertain the severity of presenting problems and also serve as objective measures of progress in therapy.

List of validated measures

- Beck Anxiety Inventory (BAI): Beck, Epstein, Brown & Steer, 1988
- Beck Depression Inventory (BDI): Beck et al., 1961
- The Symptom Checklist 90-R (SCL-90-R): Derogatis, 1977
- Fear Questionnaire: Marks & Mathews, 1979
- The Anxiety Disorders Interview Schedule-Revised (ADIS-R): DiNardo & Barlow, 1988
- The Yale-Brown Obsessive Compulsive Scale (Y-BOCS): Goodman et al., 1989

A timeline of events can help clarify the interrelationships between the presenting problems, as well as reveal the issues that are having the most significant impact on mood and functioning. It can also clarify the precipitating factors. The timeline should include previous attempts to treat the problem, both medical and psychological. Clients' past experience of psychopharmacological and/ or psychological treatment will affect their view of their effectiveness and their decision to pursue your treatment suggestions. Assess whether they found past treatment helpful or unhelpful and why. It can also be useful to ascertain why they are seeking assistance now.

Assessing risk

The presence of any psychiatric disorder is a risk factor for suicidal behaviour. A recent longitudinal study has found that the presence of any anxiety disorder is significantly associated with suicidal ideation and attempts (Sareen et al., 2005). The study also found that the risk is higher for people who have co-morbid anxiety and mood disorders in comparison with those with a mood disorder alone. Therefore, an essential component of any psychological assessment is ascertaining if the client is at risk of harming themself or others.

Assessing risk involves asking direct questions about suicidal thoughts and behaviours. Asking about suicide does not create risk in people who do not have suicidal thoughts and there is no evidence to suggest that it increases the likelihood of suicide attempts. It is important to ask questions in a calm, comfortable, and non-judgemental manner to assist the client to openly discuss issues related to suicide and self-harm.

To begin the discussion, it is helpful to ask open-ended questions like:

"Sometimes when people feel very anxious or down, they have thoughts of hurting themselves or of suicide. What has been your experience?"

"What sort of thoughts have you had?"

Once you have established that the client has or has had suicidal thoughts or attempts, it is necessary to ask more specific questions to ascertain their current level of risk.

The current level of risk is determined by assessing the presence of risk factors and protective factors. Risk factors increase the probability of a certain outcome occurring and protective factors decrease the likelihood of a negative outcome occurring.

The main risk factors for suicidal behaviour are:

- A history of serious suicide attempts—the level of seriousness relates to the lethality of the method, whether any attempt was made to prevent discovery, how much planning was involved, whether substance abuse was involved, and the reason(s) the attempt failed.
- Current intent to die—often people who attempt suicide do not want to die; they report that they just want relief, a way to escape their pain.
- The presence of a plan—assess the viability of the plan, how detailed the plan is, whether they have already started to prepare for the attempt (writing a will, suicide note, giving their belongings away).
- Access to the means to carry out their plan, i.e., stockpiled pills, access to firearms, weapons.
- Little or no social support.
- A sense of hopelessness.
- Substance abuse and intoxication.
- Recent significant losses.
- Serious physical illness.
- The presence of one or more psychiatric disorders.
- History of violence.
- Client's family history of suicide.

Protective factors include:

- A sense of connection to others.
- The presence of a caring partner.
- A sense of responsibility to others (to children, partner, colleagues).
- Social supports and resources.
- Strong beliefs against suicide (e.g., moral or religious).
- Positive attitude toward treatment and motivation to pursue treatment.
- Stated plans for the future (e.g., dentist appointment, child visitation, going to school).

Once you have more information about the client's risk and protective factors, you can make a decision regarding their level of risk and the level of care they need. If you find it difficult to ascertain the level of risk or how to best manage the situation, it is recommended that contact be made with a suitably trained mental health clinician for advice. It is good practice to consult another appropriately trained clinician when managing risk, as this can provide protection and peace of mind and can enable you to continue treatment in an effective manner.

Generally, if the client has suicidal ideation, a viable plan, and intent to die, they need immediate intervention to ensure their safety. This may involve hospitalisation and it will be necessary to notify appropriate services to implement the plan for containment and treatment. If the client expresses ideation and has a plan but they have no intent, they are likely to need immediate support, but this may be provided without hospitalisation, particularly if they have adequate social supports. Again, notify appropriate services to access care. Clients who have suicidal thoughts but no plan or intent should continue to be monitored and assessed over time.

It can be helpful to suggest that the client dispose of any potentially dangerous items like pills or weapons. Some therapists advocate using a "no suicide" contract with their clients; however, this may give therapists a false sense of comfort that leads to inadequate assessment of risk factors. Although it may be useful, a contract should not replace a thorough risk assessment or ongoing monitoring and assessments.

Assessing clients' risk of violence towards others is also important. Again, ask direct questions about violent or homicidal thoughts towards others. If they express violent thoughts towards a specific person or people and have a plan and intent, it is important to notify appropriate agencies. It is also important for the therapist to carefully consider their own safety when working with people who display aggressive behaviour or have a history of violence. In this case, the therapy environment should have easy access to assistance—it is not advisable to be the sole clinician in a building when treating clients that present with a risk of harm to others.

The therapist should protect their personal information, such as private address and contact details from clients. If a client makes threats towards a therapist, then it is appropriate to terminate the therapeutic relationship. Again, it is recommended that therapists seek supervision or consultation with another appropriately trained clinician when managing risk of violence.

Precipitating factors

Precipitating factors are usually real or perceived situations or events (as well as interpretations of events) that may have triggered the presenting issue(s). If the client presents several issues, one or more of the presenting issues may, in fact, be a precipitating factor. As in the scenario above, ongoing relationship difficulties may have led to increased alcohol use resulting in a drinking problem or ongoing anxiety about the relationship may have led to a panic attack. Precipitating factors involve events and situations like losses, trauma, life changes, or conflict, as well as how the client perceived or interpreted the events.

Make sure to assess cognitions as well as feelings, behaviours, and events. Precipitating factors may also include overuse of over-the-counter and prescribed medication (e.g., cold medicine, diet pills, codeine, SSRIs, anti-inflammatories), illicit substances (e.g., speed, cocaine, hallucinogens), and medical conditions (e.g., low blood sugar, thyroid problems, hormone imbalances, heart conditions) as they can sometimes produce anxiety symptoms. Ensure that you ask your client about any medications or substances that they have taken, as well as directing them to get a full physical check-up to exclude any organic basis to their symptoms.

Predisposing factors

Although the strategies that we discuss in this workbook are aimed at managing and resolving current issues, it is helpful to understand presenting problems within a historical context. Predisposing factors include genetic and biological vulnerabilities, as well as environmental influences.

It is important to ask about your client's family history of anxiety and other psychiatric problems including alcohol and drug abuse. A family history of psychiatric problems may not only indicate a genetic vulnerability, but also is likely to have had an environmental impact on the client. For instance, if the client's mother had untreated panic disorder with agoraphobia, she most likely modelled avoidance behaviours and the client may have lived in a state of confusion or fear. Environmental influences that can lead to anxiety difficulties are trauma, abuse or neglect, significant losses early in life, or growing up in an environment that fostered insecurity or fear and that did not model effective skills to cope with anxiety. Biological vulnerabilities generally refer to chemical imbalances in the brain, e.g., serotonin deficiency that may be caused by genetic or environmental factors. The client may have a predisposition to a chemical imbalance, they may have ingested a substance that causes the chemical changes in the brain, or they may have a medical condition that may lead to chemical changes as well as anxiety about having a medical problem.

Although it is helpful to know about any significant losses, abuse, or trauma in childhood and early adulthood (recent events would be classed as precipitating factors, but it is important to consider the cumulative effect of stress over time), it is not necessary or recommended to ask about the details of trauma or abuse as this may re-traumatise the client and lead to further mood or behavioural disturbances. If the client begins to discuss the details with you during the assessment phase, gently explain to him or her that talking in detail about their experiences may lead to further distress and it may not be wise to do so at this stage.

Maintaining factors

Maintaining factors to anxiety problems are usually behaviours or cognitions that make people more vulnerable to stress and that continue the cycle of anxiety. Behaviours that can maintain anxiety problems include lifestyle factors like disturbed sleeping and eating patterns, alcohol or drug use, employment and financial issues, and lack of social supports and interactions. Furthermore, avoidance behaviours are very common among people with anxiety and generally maintain the problem or disorder. Thought patterns that often contribute to the maintenance of anxiety are constant worrying, rumination, catastrophising, misinterpreting symptoms, and guilt or stigma-inducing thoughts.

Having anxiety problems may also fulfil some needs, and these needs may also be maintaining factors for the anxiety. For instance, when people are unwell, others may be more caring and supportive than usual, and people may spend more time and do more for them. If your client believes they may lose the attention and support of others if they improve, then they are likely to be ambivalent about change.

Protective factors and strengths

Protective factors are the internal and external resources that help the client to cope and that will support them through making the necessary changes to improve their quality of life. Internal resources include positive characteristics, cognitions and beliefs like intelligence, humour, insight, good judgement, self-esteem, and hopefulness. External resources refer mainly to community and social supports, family relationships, and stable accommodation, employment, and finances. Assess your client's opinion of his or her own strengths—not being able to communicate personal strengths speaks volumes about the client's level of self-esteem.

Current coping mechanisms

Coping mechanisms include both adaptive and maladaptive cognitions and behaviours that assist people to manage their discomfort and distress.

	Coping mechanisms
Maladaptive	• Avoid places, people, situations, or things that cause discomfort or anxiety • Binge-eat • Use alcohol or drugs • Bottle up emotions • Fight emotions • Berate self for feeling anxious • Stay in bed all day • Deliberate self-harm/suicidal behaviour
Adaptive	• Try to find a solution • Talk to a friend • Obtain more information about the problem • Talk yourself through anxiety-provoking situations • Face fears • Accept emotions • Exercise • Do relaxation exercises • Distract self • Listen to soothing music

Formulation

The information you gather in the assessment phase will allow you to make a formulation of your client's current presenting problems as well as determine an appropriate treatment plan and/or referral options. If you do decide to refer on, Handout 2.1 provides education about psychological treatment and what to expect from a therapist.

Example formulation:

Predisposing factors:
Harry reports having a pleasant childhood, however, acknowledges that his mother experienced some persistent anxiety, and that he was quite close to his mother. Harry did quite well in his schooling, and mixed with children of his age, but also felt like a bit of an outsider at this time.

Precipitating factors:
When aged 21, after several unsatisfactory positions of employment, Harry found a job that he felt enthusiastic about and happy with. At this time he had a serious car accident that required a lengthy hospitalisation and rehabilitation

for an injured leg. Upon recovering from this injury he experienced a panic attack initially when travelling, and then began to severely restrict outings.

Presenting problems:
Harry, now aged 23, with some prompting from his sister, has acknowledged that his anxiety has severely restricted his life. He feels that if he does not address this problem now, he will not be able to have employment or social relationships in the future.

Maintaining factors:
Factors that maintain anxiety and present barriers to treatment are his avoidance behaviours, ongoing chronic pain from his injury, regular use of large quantities of alcohol, low self-confidence, and a somewhat negative view of himself.

Strengths and protective factors:
Harry is quite intelligent and has previous experience of satisfactory and successful employment. While he is not confident socially, he has a pleasant and witty personality, and good social skills.

Coping mechanisms:
Current coping mechanisms include avoidance of anxiety-provoking situations, talking to his sister, and use of alcohol and prescription medication.

Values, priorities, and goals:
Anxiety treatment is a high priority for Harry, as he recognises that the anxiety has prevented him from pursuing most activities that he values.

Clinician's assessment tool

Presenting problem:

- Open questions (What has brought you here today? Can you tell me a little about what's been happening for you?)
- Have you tried to get help for this particular problem before—how was it helpful or unhelpful?
- Why now? What is making you want to do something about this issue now?

Specific anxiety assessment:

- Describe the first time this happened (when, where, symptoms, etc.)
- Triggers for anxiety (people, places, situations)
- What do you fear might happen?
- Have there been times when the problem has been better or worse?
- When more likely to occur?
- What are the exceptions? (when you would have expected anxiety or avoidance to occur but person was able to manage the symptoms/situation)
- Are there factors that help you with this problem? Coping mechanisms?
- What do you avoid to prevent anxiety?
- What does it stop you from doing?
- Describe a recent time this has occurred—include what happened, when, what you were feeling and thinking before, during, and after experience and what you did

Risk assessment:

Consider the presence of dangerous behaviours such as suicidality, criminal behaviour, or violence. Review the following factors of such behaviours.

- Past behaviour: frequency, triggers, severity or lethality, impulsivity
- Current plan, intent and means
- Level of hopelessness
- Protective factors: internal and external resources

(If high risk, review safety of treatment setting, ensure other professionals are engaged in treatment team, refer to more specialised service if appropriate, develop a plan with client to cope with any imminent risks to client or others should they arise.)

Essential facts:

- Health and development in early childhood
- Family environment and relationship with parents and siblings (include genogram and family history of mental health problems)
- School and work history
- Substance use history
- Relationship history
- Traumas, accidents, and grief
- Ability to manage daily living skills, self-care, finances, social relationships
- Physical health and current medication for both physical and mental health issues

Formulation:

Include presenting problem, predisposing, precipitating, maintaining and protective factors, coping mechanisms, values, priorities and goals, and recommended treatment.

Assessing the barriers to therapy for your client

Readiness for therapy

It is also important to assess if psychological treatment is appropriate taking into account not only the presenting problem and symptoms but the person's current level of functioning and motivation. Consider the following factors in ascertaining the client's suitability for psychological treatment at this time:

- Can they concentrate?
- Are they too activated or fatigued?
- Do they require psychopharmacological medication first?
- Do they think they have a problem?
- Are they looking for a quick fix?
- Do they have a positive attitude toward psychological treatment or do they have a more medical model?

If the client's level of anxiety or depression is very severe, they are likely to be too distressed, hopeless, unmotivated, agitated, restless, or fatigued to commence therapy. It may be useful to consider pharmacological treatment to alleviate the intensity of symptoms so that the client is able to participate effectively in therapy. Also, if the client's basic needs are not being met, e.g., not getting adequate sleep, nutrition, not taking showers, then the focus of treatment would be to address these issues first. Maslow's hierarchy of needs (1954) depicts the necessity for basic needs to be met before higher functioning goals can be achieved.

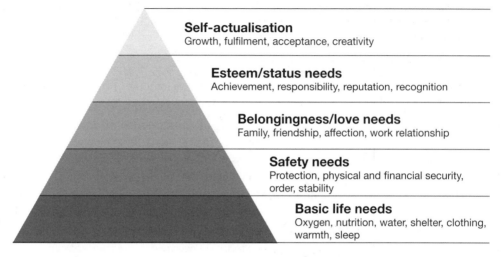

Figure 2: Maslow's hierarchy of needs (1954)

Most people with mental health problems do not receive or seek help (Andrews, Hall, Teesson & Henderson, 1999; Kessler et al., 2005), so the fact that the client has made it to your office and is discussing their problems with you demonstrates some level of motivation and desire for change. It can be helpful to acknowledge this and how difficult it may be for them to discuss their current problems.

Stages of change

Research by Prochaska and DiClemente (1983) describes people's readiness for change according to what stage of change they are in currently. There are five stages in this theory: the *precontemplative*, the *contemplative*, the *planning and preparation* stage, the *action* stage, and the *maintenance* stage. The *precontemplative* stage of change occurs when people are not considering change at the moment, they are not overly distressed by their feelings or behaviour, and do not currently feel the need to make changes in their lives. The *contemplative* stage is when people are just starting to think about making changes but they are not currently taking any action towards any goals. The *planning and preparation* stage is when people start taking some active steps towards change by collecting information about what they might do and preparing to take the necessary steps. The *action* stage is when they are currently actively making changes and working towards their goals. Finally, the *maintenance* stage is when people have achieved their goals and are maintaining the change long-term, for at least six months.

Prochaska and DiClemente's stages of change do not necessarily occur in a linear process—in fact, people may move freely and easily among the various stages. Clients will most often approach a health practitioner during the *planning and preparation* stage or *action* stage. However, you may see people who are actually in the *precontemplative* stage—these are often people who come in due to pressure from others.

It can be helpful to assess what stage your client may be at in order to ascertain their readiness for therapy in general, as well as their readiness for the various processes of therapy (Prochaska & Norcross, 2001). One way to gauge current motivation is to ask your client to list the pros and cons of their behaviour (or of changing their behaviour, or of commencing treatment—whichever is most suitable to the situation). If they are listing many more advantages to their behaviour than disadvantages, or they believe that the impact of the advantages are more important than the disadvantages, then this is a good indicator that your client is at least ambivalent about changing.

If your client perceives more benefits from staying the same rather than changing, they may not be amenable to ongoing therapy. It can still be helpful at this stage to review information about maintaining emotional health and acknowledging the individual's strengths, coping mechanisms, and vulnerabilities. Providing information about relevant difficulties and the options for appropriate treatment as well as conveying realistic hope that change is possible can also be helpful. Once they have this information, the client will be better informed when or if they next find themselves in a more active stage of change.

Other barriers to psychological treatment

Stigma

Many people affected by psychological difficulties are influenced by a mark of disapproval from others or a sense of shame about their inability to cope or "to be normal," called stigma. Feeling embarrassed or ashamed can prevent people from approaching family members, friends, or health professionals for assistance. It may have taken your client many weeks, months, or even years to talk to someone about their problem and even then they may be reluctant to accept medical or psychological treatment because of ideas that only "crazy" people need medication or therapy. It can be helpful to discuss the fact that stigma about mental health issues and treatment are common, and ask your client if they have any self-stigmatising beliefs—or have heard others make comments that are unsupportive or stigmatising—that may get in the way of pursuing recommended treatment.

It can be helpful to discuss how the lack of knowledge among the general public about mental health problems leads to stigma, and point out how recent efforts to raise awareness about depression has led to a decreased level of stigma. It is also useful to make comparisons between physical health problems (like heart disease or diabetes) and mental health problems—that they are both affected by genetic, biological, and environmental influences, they both require treatment and ongoing management, effective treatment is available, and affected individuals can reduce their vulnerability through attending to lifestyle factors like nutrition, sleep, and exercise. An open discussion about the reality of stigma related to psychological problems and treatment in our society can foster a sense of injustice about the situation, rather than leave them feeling inferior or embarrassed by their current difficulties. Worksheet 2.3 discusses the effects of stigma and ways for clients to overcome it.

Scepticism related to psychological assistance

Some clients may be sceptical about non-pharmacological methods of treatment. This may be due to negative past experiences with other therapists, or to old-fashioned or vague ideas about psychotherapy. Ensure that you assess their past treatment experiences—both medical and psychological—including who provided treatment, their method of treatment, their qualifications and experience, the negative and positive effects of treatment, and what may have contributed to these effects. In order for the client to want to pursue therapy, they need to feel confident that the practitioner is well qualified and experienced in treating people with anxiety problems, that the method of treatment is specifically suited to their difficulties, and that the techniques they will learn are known to be effective. Clients also need to know from the beginning that the process of treatment will be both supportive and challenging and will require a commitment from them to put in the necessary time, effort, and energy as well as a willingness to tolerate discomfort in order to be effective. Again, it is very powerful and helpful if you can demonstrate within the first session that change is possible, for instance, by teaching clients a simple deep breathing exercise that immediately demonstrates that they can learn skills to reduce their level of anxiety.

Don't have enough time or money

Reviewing all options for treatment and realistically looking at financial outlay as an investment in their future can be helpful. Reviewing priorities can also be helpful when considering that some consistent amount of time and energy will be required to complete a programme of therapy. Individuals may feel over-burdened by obligations to others, so that they feel they cannot afford to spend time on therapy. It is important to consider the likely outcomes of therapy and that improvements will benefit not only the individuals themselves but are also likely to result in some improved functioning in their other roles. It can be helpful to consider the cost of not addressing the anxiety problem.

Be the therapist or refer on?

Depending on your own interests, experience, and expertise, you may feel that someone else would be better suited to provide therapy to your client. Knowing when to refer on is an important part of the assessment. Consider the following factors when making the decision to treat the client yourself or to refer the client to someone else.

- level of rapport with client
- likelihood of client taking up treatment with someone else
- affordability of other options in relation to treatment with you
- your level of interest in providing therapy
- whether you have the time and support necessary to treat the client within your current role
- the complexity of the client's presenting problems in relation to your ability to address their issues adequately
- the availability of supervision or support from colleagues to provide assistance when you get stuck or frustrated

Treatment planning and goal-setting

Collaborating with clients

When you think you have a good idea of what is going on and why, present your thoughts based on your assessment to your client, and at the same time give them verbal and written psychoeducation about their particular concern and relevant effective treatments. Emphasise their current strengths and resources and convey realistic optimism about their prognosis. Ask them if they agree with your formulation and what they would add or change. Be aware of cultural differences that may affect the way people view mental health problems. If there are differing views, present your rationale and at the same time be respectful and adapt your formulation to include their understanding of the problem.

Collaboration with your clients is very important in both building therapeutic rapport and increasing their motivation to pursue recommended treatment.

Your ability to engage your client and foster a strong therapeutic alliance that will motivate them to participate in the process is important in determining the outcome of therapy (Orlinsky, Grawe, & Park, 1994).

Discuss treatment options and rationale with your client and openly discuss and normalise your client's current barriers to pursuing therapy and any ambivalence towards commencing treatment.

Remember to balance presenting a hopeful view of your client's future with realistic expectations. Research shows that successfully imparting realistic hope to clients is one of the main indicators for change in therapy (Lambert, 1992). Clients need to understand that they can change, and that the techniques they will learn are well researched and effective. They also need to know that the process of therapy is not easy, that it requires work both within the sessions and between the sessions, that therapy will be both supportive and challenging, and that setbacks along the way are a normal part of the process. Ultimately, the decision to pursue therapy is up to the client.

Treatment plan

Discuss the various intervention options with your client in relation to the problems they presented and decide together where to start. Generally, starting with a behavioural intervention is recommended as they are easier to impart and provide more immediate results that are likely to motivate the client to continue therapy. However, if the client is most interested in the cognitive techniques, you may decide that pursuing these interventions will be most beneficial. Worksheet 2.1 provides a general outline of the components of a treatment plan and Worksheet 2.2 provides a means of monitoring progress.

Essential components of a treatment plan:

A goal
- What is the change that the client hopes to achieve?
- One goal at a time is the best way to approach therapy; however, improvements in other areas of functioning may occur as a means of achieving the primary goal.
- It is likely that the goal will be a substantial change from current functioning, and therefore it is helpful to break down the goal into steps. Success in the first sub-goal provides confidence for the client, and for the process of therapy.

A method of measuring change
- How can progress towards the goal be measured? It may be helpful to measure an activity, such as time spent out of the house, as well as emo-

tional functioning, such as the level of distress when going out of the house.

A method of recording practice
- This can be a simple diary or journal and includes practice in and out of the session. In order to ensure that the strategies are helpful, we need a reasonably accurate record of how and when they are being used. A sample treatment journal is available in Worksheet 2.2.

A method of noticing barriers
- Change is difficult for everyone, and many unforeseen barriers may arise. These also need to be recorded so that they can be managed; meanwhile goals can still be achieved.

Coping with repeated crises

When an individual is particularly vulnerable or experiencing severe ongoing stress, they may often be in crisis. When in a crisis state, it is very difficult to maintain work towards longer term goals and to try new and challenging tasks. It can be helpful to develop a list of simple and effective strategies to alleviate distress in times of crisis, and therefore minimise the impact of ongoing crises. Handout 2.2 discusses the components of a crisis management list. This list needs to be kept in a visible place so that it is immediately accessible. It is wise to consider attempting several distress management strategies when confronted with a crisis. It may also be helpful to involve supportive people and relevant agencies when planning for crisis management.

Psychological treatment

Psychological treatment is a non-medical method of treatment involving talking with the client(s). Psychological methods are useful both on their own and in combination with medical treatments. Issues can be addressed individually, with couples, with families, and within a group setting.

Psychological treatments can assist by:

1. Relieving symptoms associated with anxiety, panic, obsession, phobias, depression, and psychosis;
2. Helping identify early warning signs to problems and thus reduce the frequency, intensity and/or duration of setbacks and relapses;
3. Helping to increase communication, social, problem-solving, and stress management skills;
4. Increasing awareness of thoughts and beliefs that affect emotions and behaviour and helping to change unhelpful thought patterns; and
5. Providing support through a difficult period or situation (loss of job, death of loved one, relationship breakdown, coming to terms with a mental illness).

An evidence-based form of psychological intervention that addresses all the above issues is cognitive behavioural therapy (CBT). However, there are other forms of therapy that may be just as suitable or helpful. The most important aspect of therapy according to research is not the form of therapy but the strength of the relationship between the client and the therapist. Therefore, it is important to find a therapist with whom you feel comfortable and respected.

When you meet a therapist for the first time, it is okay to ask questions about his or her experience and training and the form of therapy he or she plans to use to help you address your issues. You also need to find out how often and how long you are likely to be seeing the therapist. It may take a few sessions for you to feel comfortable with the therapist. If at any time you feel unhappy with therapy or the therapist, it can often be useful to discuss your concerns with him or her. If you do not wish to do this and do not feel that therapy is progressing, you may consider seeing another therapist.

Treatment plan

Treatment goal:

_____

_____

Steps to achieving the goal (mini-goals):

_____

_____

Skills/strategies/resources required to achieve the goal:

_____

_____

_____

Estimated number of therapy sessions: _____

Agreed frequency of therapy sessions: _____

_____

Date for review of therapy progress: _____

Measuring progress

Measuring changes in behaviour—objective measure:

_____

_____

Measuring changes in emotional experience and level of distress—objective and subjective measures:

_____

_____

_____

Treatment journal

Date	Task/skill practised e.g. relaxation exercise or exposure task of going to the shops	Measure of emotional distress before practise e.g. rating of units of distress	Measure of emotional distress after practise	Measure of behaviour change e.g. times per day leaving the house	Barriers to treatment tasks/ practise e.g. illness, higher level of fear, unexpected workload

Stigma

What is stigma?

Stigma is a mark of shame, disgrace, or disapproval. Unfortunately, stigma is often encountered in relation to mental health problems such as anxiety, depression, and psychosis. These attitudes to mental health issues are unrealistic, unhelpful, and can prevent people from finding help and solutions for emotional difficulties and mental illness. This is especially clear considering that researchers have estimated that about half of us will meet the criteria for a mental disorder at some time in our lives. This worksheet assists in understanding, identifying, and protecting against the effects of stigma.

Why does it happen?

It is caused by a lack of understanding and knowledge due to widespread stereo-types and myths circulated by individuals, groups, and the media.

How does it work?

The lack of knowledge by others about the targeted group causes people to behave as if the stereotypes and myths are true, e.g., they withdraw, tease, reject, fear, avoid.

↓

Stigma is internalised by those who are targeted (aged, unemployed, migrants, people with mental illnesses, people who are HIV+) causing them to feel bad about themselves.

↓

Due to fear of stigma, individuals do not share their experiences with others.

↓

Because true and valid experiences and stories are not shared, people remain igno-rant and stigma continues.

Treating Stress and Anxiety © 2008 Crown House Publishing and Dr Lillian Nejad and Katerina Volny

What are some common myths associated with mental health problems?

Participants reported the following myths (written verbatim):

Myth/stereotype	Reality
1. That everyone needs to be hospitalised.	The majority of people are not hospitalised.
2. If you have mental illness, you've lost your intelligence (you're nuts).	Mental health problems like anxiety or depression can affect your concentration and memory temporarily, but you do not lose your intelligence.
3. That you can snap out of it.	It is not a matter of willpower. Access to psychological and medical treatment is important.
4. It will keep happening over and over.	Setbacks are a normal part of recovery. However, there are ways to reduce their frequency, duration, and intensity.
5. I'll never be able to change.	It is common for people to feel hopeless especially if they have been experiencing difficulties for a long time. However, change is possible, and just like physical problems, treatment is available to assist in overcoming mental health problems.

What are the effects of stigma on society?

As part of previous groups people with mental health problems, participants were asked how society treated them due to the effects of stigma. They made the following statements:

- "This person is not like other people"   Marginalisation
- "I don't want to hang around you"   Discrimination
- "Something is wrong with that person"   Humiliation
- "People don't listen to you"   Condescension

Have you encountered some instances of stigma?

-

-

-

-

-

What are the consequences of stigma for those who are targeted?

The following consequences to stigma have been reported by people experiencing mental health problems:

- Lack of understanding
- Lack of motivation
- Generalised apathy because you are struggling with society
- Frustration
- Stress
- Feel weighed down
- Isolation
- Confusion
- Inertia because you can't change what society thinks
- Anger
- Withdrawal

Have you experienced consequences of stigma?

-
-
-
-

What are some ways to protect yourself against the effects of stigma?

The following are some tips to help increase your confidence and help you to recover:

- Have a holistic view of yourself as an individual with strengths and vulnerabilities—you are more than your anxiety!
- Set realistic goals for yourself and reward yourself for your accomplishments.
- If you are stuck, get some help. Counsellors, GPs, family members, and friends are some of the people who may be able to help, encourage, or guide you to reach your goals.
- Make time to relax and have time out. Keeping stress levels down is important—you need time on your own to collect your thoughts and "take a breather".
- Participate in activities that you enjoy or once enjoyed. Don't wait to feel motivated—this will come after you do something, not before.
- Respect yourself by taking care of yourself and by appreciating who you are.

Treating Stress and Anxiety © 2008 Crown House Publishing and Dr Lillian Nejad and Katerina Volny

What are you going to do?

1.

2.

What can you do about stigma?

Suggestions of ways to help reduce stigma in society:

- Educate people
- Correct people
- Be aware of your own stereotypes
- Join advocacy groups like NAMI or SANE
- Learn more about your illness
- Share your experiences with others (family, friends, others with mental health issues, clinicians)
- Challenge false statements made by others

Where can you get more information about stigma and dispelling common myths and stereotypes?

By increasing your knowledge about mental illness, you can educate others. One of the easiest ways to access information is on the internet. The following websites have helpful information about stigma and common myths about mental illness:

- <http://www.sane.org> click on 'StigmaWatch'
- <http://www.nmha.org/infoctr/factsheets/14.cfm> US National Mental Health Association's factsheet on stigma and myths of mental illness

Worksheet 2.3   Page 4 of 4

Coping with repeated crises

Sometimes people experience high levels of distress on a regular basis. It can help to plan for these times by writing a list of coping strategies that is easily accessible during a crisis. Keep in mind that the purpose of these strategies is not to make you feel better (although this may occur), but to get you through the crisis.

Make sure that you plan strategies that suit you and are easy for you to do. The strategies below are just suggestions. Don't try things for the first time in a crisis; instead, practise new skills or strategies when you are feeling well so they come more naturally during crises.

Remember to:
- Set a goal of getting through the next few minutes
- When distressing thoughts distract you, keep bringing yourself back to the strategy you are using
- Plan to do several strategies in a row

Calming strategies
- Do a breathing or relaxation exercise
- Take a bath
- Pat your cat or dog
- Go to a pleasant place
- Listen to soothing music

Distracting strategies
- Watch a favourite TV show or DVD
- Sing along to songs on the radio
- Do a hobby or work task
- Do some cooking, housework, or gardening
- Describe a painting in your house in detail

Active strategies
- Make yourself a cup of tea
- Do a hobby or work task
- Do some cooking, housework, or gardening
- Do some exercise (walking, cycling, yoga, swimming)
- Do something with or for a family member or friend

Support strategies
- Talk to a supportive friend or family member
- Do something with or for a family member or friend
- Use a phone helpline
- Make an appointment with a counsellor or other helpful person

Thinking strategies
- Replace unhelpful thoughts with helpful thoughts. Some examples are:

    "High levels of distress only last for a short time—it will pass."
    "I have been in a similar situation before and survived."
    "I'll be in a better position to solve problems when the distress has passed."

Treating Stress and Anxiety © 2008 Crown House Publishing and Dr Lillian Nejad and Katerina Volny

Chapter 3

Treatment for anxiety disorders

In recent years there has been an increase in literature and tools aimed at disseminating information about evidence-based treatment. There are many sources of evidence-based treatment guidelines that provide analysis and synthesis of the vast amount of research into anxiety disorders. These sources often provide both detailed treatment guidelines for professionals and a summary of treatment guidelines for clients seeking treatment. We have reviewed evidence-based guidelines for the treatment of a range of anxiety disorders to provide a guide outlining the most appropriate treatment for each disorder (see Table 3 overleaf for summary).

Cognitive therapy

Cognitive therapy is based on the theory that emotions are preceded by thoughts and influenced by core beliefs (Beck, 1975; Ellis, Harper & Powers, 1975). Thoughts that lead to extreme emotions are often unrealistic, exaggerated, and unhelpful. Identifying the thoughts that lead to extreme emotions and modifying these thoughts can, in turn, reduce the distress associated with the thoughts. Additional strategies to manage thoughts such as distraction from persistent thoughts, managing persistent thoughts, and preventing rumination are also helpful.

Behavioural therapy

Behavioural therapy is based on research about learning through modelling, reward, reinforcement, and punishment. The idea is that current maladaptive behaviours have been learned and they can be unlearned through a variety of behavioural tasks including exposure to feared stimuli, relaxation and breathing exercises, behavioural experiments, distraction, and response prevention (Skinner, 1938, 1953; Watson, 1913).

Guidelines for anxiety treatment (McIntosh et al., 2004) recommend that cognitive behavioural therapy should be delivered by suitably trained and supervised professionals who adhere to evidence-based treatment protocols. Weekly sessions of one to two hours are recommended and treatment is to be completed within four months of commencement. McIntosh et al. (2004) recommend that persons suffering from anxiety disorders should be offered the

Table 3: Summary of treatment guidelines

Disorder	CBT psychotherapy	Medication	Other effective strategies
Panic disorder[1]	CBT has longest duration of effect. 7–14 hours of treatment recommended.	Benzodiazepines not recommended. SSRI medication effective.	Self-help based on CBT principles has lesser effectiveness.
Generalised anxiety disorder[2]	CBT has longest duration of effect. More effective than benzos, analytic or non-directive psychotherapy, and placebo. 16–20 hours of treatment recommended.	Benzodiazepines no longer than 2–4 weeks. SSRI medication effective.	Self-help based on CBT principles has lesser effectiveness.
Post-traumatic stress disorder[3]	CBT effective	Medication in combination with CBT for more severe PTSD. SSRIs have been found to be more effective for hyperarousal and numbing/avoidant symptoms than re-experiencing trauma.	
Obsessive compulsive disorder[4]	Lower relapse rates following treatment cessation for exposure and response prevention CBT compared to clomipramine medication.	Clomipramine and SSRIs.	
Specific phobia	Behaviour therapy (exposure with or without relaxation training)		
Social phobia[5]	Combination of CBT and medication most effective with lower relapse rates.	SSRIs are effective.	

[1]Ballenger et al., 1998; McIntosh et al., 2004.
[2]Ballenger, 2001; McIntosh et al., 2004.
[3]Foa, Hearst-Ikeda & Perry, 1995; Stanley & Turner, 1995; Brady et al., 2000; Brunello et al., 2001; Davidson, 2000.
[4]Foa et al., 2005; Greist et al., 1995; Marks et al., 1980; Stein, Spandaccini & Hollander, 1995.
[5]Bruce & Saeed, 1999; Brunello et al., 2000; Lydiard, 2001.

full range of treatments that demonstrate effectiveness and that for personal preference they may choose a treatment with lesser effectiveness.

Cognitive behavioural therapy

Cognitive behavioural therapy (CBT) has been established as an effective treatment for anxiety disorders. CBT, pioneered by Albert Ellis and Aaron Beck, is based on the theory that thoughts are the main influence on emotions and behaviour and, more specifically, that the interpretation of events rather than events themselves lead to emotional and behavioural responses. Therefore, if an interpretation of an event is inaccurate, irrational, or exaggerated, the result is often extreme and distressing emotions and dysfunctional behaviours.

Components of CBT for anxiety

Psychoeducation
Education about anxiety and effective treatment provides the client with an understanding of the disorder and a rationale to commence psychological and/or medical treatment. Increased knowledge generally reduces fear, increases a sense of control and hope for positive change, and in turn increases the commitment to treatment.

Homework
Homework is a fundamental aspect of CBT in both the assessment and treatment phases of therapy. Self-monitoring thoughts and then recording them is one of the most useful homework tasks and is usually assigned in the early stages of therapy. Clients are encouraged to write down important aspects of a problem immediately after it occurs to ensure the record is as accurate as possible.

Self-monitoring also has a therapeutic effect. For instance, research shows that just writing down the experience of panic right after the experience of it can help people recover from panic disorder. A diary or thought record can also help bring clarity to the precipitants and maintaining factors of problem thoughts, feelings, and behaviours. Therapy involves a variety of other cognitive and behavioural homework assignments including reading psychoeducation, disputing cognitions, participating in behavioural experiments, practising relaxation exercises, and exposure tasks. It is important for clients to be oriented to the importance of homework in the treatment of their anxiety problem or disorder. If clients do not complete assignments, it is essential to assess the barriers to doing the homework and agree on how these barriers can be overcome. Common barriers are they didn't understand the homework, they forgot to do it, it was too confronting or embarrassing, or they have trouble reading and writing. Work together to creatively come up with solutions, e.g., they call you if they don't understand, they post reminders around the house, they record their homework on tape rather than in writing, etc.

Other notable treatment options

Medication

Medication is a method of treatment for anxiety disorders. This text focuses on psychological aspects of treatment and does not provide expert information about psychopharmacological treatment. Table 3 provides an indication of how medication may complement or contrast with psychological treatment. It is noted that psychological treatments have generally been found to have longer lasting effects than a course of medication. In general, medication is more appropriate when more severe symptoms of anxiety are present to moderate symptoms or when only minimal impairment in functioning is present. The individual's preferences and availability of cognitive behaviour therapy are important considerations when considering the use of medication. Clients who are having difficulty in completing treatment tasks due to the severity of their anxiety symptoms may benefit from short-term psychopharmacological intervention.

If considering the use of medication as a standalone or supplementary treatment for anxiety disorders consult a medical practitioner, psychiatrist, or specialised texts that describe the latest medication guidelines in more detail. When medication is used, keep in mind that in order for important aspects of cognitive behaviour therapy to be effective, the individual must experience some anxiety symptoms, rather than have the symptoms completely ameliorated by the use of medication. If a client has been on medication throughout the duration of treatment, it can be useful to recommend some booster sessions when they are no longer on medication.

Hypnosis

Hypnosis is a method of treatment for anxiety disorders. This text does not provide expert information about hypnosis; however, the following is a brief explanation of the process and uses. Hypnosis is a technique that utilises instructions or suggestions to influence an individual's thoughts, perceptions, feelings, and behaviour. It can occur in the form of communication from one individual to another, or an individual can learn to undertake self-hypnosis. Initially a phase of "hypnotic induction" occurs where the individual is instructed to focus on his or her own thoughts and feelings. In a therapeutic setting hypnosis is used to assist individuals to relax and improve their coping mechanisms in otherwise stressful situations, or to take on different perceptions, thoughts, and behaviours to alter experiences. Hypnosis may work well in combination with "imaginal exposure" in order to imagine in detail the experience of coping with a difficult situation successfully. Hypnosis has been found to be an effective relaxation method, and is often used to manage the experience of pain and discomfort during medical and dental procedures and childbirth, among other applications.

More information about hypnosis in a range of contexts is available online from the British Psychological Society in their text *The Nature of Hypnosis* (March 2001). You can also refer to the text, *Healing Scripts: Using Hypnosis to Treat Trauma and Stress* (Hunter, 2007), for interventions specific to trauma and stress.

Overview of the process of anxiety treatment

	Treatment tasks	Resources
1	Conduct an assessment and an emotional health check-up to identify whether there are any major barriers for reasonable physical and emotional health.	Clinician's Assessment Tool Worksheet 4.1 Emotional Health Check-up
2	Provide education about anxiety. Develop an understanding of the natural process of anxiety and the role that avoidance plays, clarify goals to eliminate extreme chronic anxiety, but also note that some anxiety is a natural and unavoidable part of life and we must be able to manage and tolerate it.	Handout 1.3 What is Anxiety? Handout 1.4 The Effects of Anxiety Worksheet 2.1 Treatment Plan Worksheet 2.2 Treatment Journal
3	Teach relaxation and breathing exercises to manage anxiety. Note that relaxation is incompatible with anxiety—you can't be both anxious and relaxed at same time. Relaxation is a skill and will take regular practise at non-anxiety-provoking times before being useful at anxiety-provoking times. Practise twice a day for one week, and once a day for the following four weeks.	Handout 5.1 The Purpose of Relaxation Exercises Handout 5.2 Guidelines for Relaxation Handout 5.3 Types of Relaxation Exercises CD Relaxation Techniques to Reduce Stress and Anxiety

4	Teach cognitive strategies to manage anxiety-provoking thoughts.	Handout 6.1 Thoughts, Emotions, and Behaviour: How They Work Together Worksheet 6.1 Detecting Unhelpful Thoughts Handout 6.2 Challenging Unhelpful Thoughts Worksheet 6.2 Transforming Your Unhelpful Thoughts to Helpful Thoughts
5	Develop a hierarchy of anxiety-provoking tasks. Each task must be undertaken regularly and repeatedly. The individual must stay in the anxiety-provoking situation until her anxiety decreases each time.	Handout 7.1 Why is it Important to Face Your Fears? Worksheet 7.1 Preparing to Face Your Fear Worksheet 7.2 Monitoring Your Fear
6	The client will be able to tolerate these situations without experiencing substantial anxiety. Triggers and early warning signs should be reviewed in order to plan helpful strategies for times of increased stress in the future.	Handout 8.1 List of Possible Triggers, Early Warning Signs, and Strategies Handout 8.2 Preventing Relapse Worksheet 8.1 Prevention Plan

Additional notes:

- Typically, the process for anxiety treatment would occur over seven to twenty hour-long weekly or fortnightly treatment sessions.
- There is evidence to suggest that Step 5 (exposure therapy) can be undertaken earlier in the process without necessarily having developed skills of relaxation and cognitive strategies in Steps 3 and 4.
- When working with clients with complex needs, such as those with co-morbid Axis I and/or Axis II disorders, it is appropriate to adjust the pace of therapy as treatment is likely to take longer, and be on the lookout for obstacles, barriers, and difficulties that the client may be having with each step. Treatment goals and strategies may have to be modified as more is ascertained about the client's functioning.

Considerations for cognitive behaviour therapy for anxiety disorders

Panic disorder with and without agoraphobia

Education regarding the nature of anxiety and panic attacks is a crucial component of therapy for panic disorder. It is important for the client to understand that the distressing physical experiences of a panic attack, such as hyperventilation, are not harmful in themselves. A common fear is that the panic attack is a symptom of a serious medical or psychiatric problem. People often report that they think they are having a heart attack or that they are going crazy. Because anxiety can be symptomatic of a medical problem, requesting a medical review is necessary prior to commencing psychological treatment.

Assisting the client to accept rather than fight their distressing panic symptoms through cognitive restructuring, helping them employ skills such as breathing and relaxation techniques to manage panic symptoms, and exposure therapy, are the main components of treatment for panic disorder. Self-monitoring by writing down the experience of panic right after the experience is both an effective assessment tool and treatment for panic disorder. A primary aim of this therapy is not only to reduce the experience and severity of panic attacks, but to reduce their impact on the client's functioning by changing the client's view of anxiety from a fearful and out of control experience to a more normal and functional one that they can manage with confidence. This can be achieved through helping clients learn to accept and tolerate their physical and cognitive symptoms and then use behavioural and cognitive techniques to reduce symptoms. A method of exposure therapy known as interoceptive desensitisation which involves inducing panic symptoms is a particularly useful technique that has been shown to help decrease the fear associated with the experience of panic (Barlow & Craske, 1989). An even more 'provocative' approach to treatment involves asking clients to generate and encourage symptoms and reduce the use of coping measures to manage symptoms (see Wilson (2003) for more information about this approach).

If a client presents with panic disorder with agoraphobia, education regarding the role of avoidance in maintaining their disorder is necessary. Exposure therapy is the primary mode of treatment for agoraphobia.

It is important to note that studies indicate that including family members in treatment rather than treating the client alone leads to more significant gains for the client on measures of agoraphobia (Barlow, O'Brien & Last, 1984) as well as continued improvement during the first year after therapy (Cerny, Barlow, Craske & Himadi, 1987).

Generalised anxiety disorder (GAD)

Persons with this disorder present with difficulties in limiting worry regarding a large range of concerns in their life, as well as physical symptoms such as muscle tension, sleep disturbance, and restlessness. People with GAD need to learn to distinguish between adaptive and maladaptive worries and ways to manage both. Both cognitive (cognitive restructuring, problem solving, and managing thoughts to prevent rumination) and behavioural strategies (self-monitoring, relaxation, and breathing techniques) are helpful for people with GAD.

Post-traumatic stress disorder (PTSD)

Treatment of PTSD primarily constitutes psychoeducation about common responses to trauma, learning cognitive and behavioural skills to cope with these responses, and exposure to the trauma via a variety of means including discussion, imagery, role-play, and prolonged exposure to avoided situations (Foa, Davidson & Frances, 1999; Foa, Rothbaum, Riggs & Murdock, 1991). Note that exposure (including discussion of the trauma in detail) is not recommended for particularly vulnerable individuals with complex presentations of PTSD who have a history of repeated trauma and/or abuse or neglect and display self-harm behaviours, as they may not have the coping skills necessary to tolerate the distress. Consider the following question when planning treatment: Does the individual have the resources and coping skills to tolerate the increase in distress that the initial stages of exposure therapy will evoke? If not, then treatment should focus primarily on building coping and distress tolerance skills as well as increasing supports and pleasurable activities before considering exposure tasks. Although the techniques described in this manual are relevant to PTSD (exposure, relaxation, cognitive strategies), treating PTSD is complex and requires a great deal of expertise. Therefore, a referral to a clinician that specialises in treating PTSD is recommended.

Acute stress disorder

Individuals suffering from a brief episode of anxiety and distress following a threatening event often recover well using existing coping mechanisms, and treatment is not necessarily recommended at this stage. Education about anxiety and stress responses, normalisation of anxiety and stress responses, and assisting the individual to make use of their existing coping resources is more appropriate and helpful than intensive treatment in most cases.

Obsessive compulsive disorder (OCD)

Behavioural strategies like exposure and response prevention have long been shown to be essential and effective components in treating OCD (Fals-Stewart, Marks & Shafer, 1993; Foa & Goldstein, 1978; Meyer, 1966). In the purely behavioural models of treatment, the content of obsessions is regarded as irrelevant. However, cognitive strategies are becoming more prominent aspects of therapy (Menzies & De Silva, 2003; Salkovskis, 1989; van Oppen & Arntz, 1994). Both behavioural and cognitive behavioural models of treatment regard giving reassurance to clients about their obsessions (you will not die as a result of germs, you aren't going to harm anyone) as highly counterproductive. Instead, focusing on giving psychoeducation about OCD and on the goal of reducing the distress the symptoms are causing is recommended. Education, relaxation, and cognitive restructuring can facilitate client commitment to this treatment and management of symptoms of anxiety during treatment. Although some of the techniques described in this manual are relevant to OCD (exposure, relaxation, cognitive strategies), treating OCD is complex and requires a great deal of expertise. Therefore, a referral to a clinician that specialises in treating OCD is recommended. For more information about treating OCD, refer to Menzies and De Silva's *Obsessive-Compulsive Disorder: Theory, Research and Treatment* (2003) and Foa and Wilson's *Stop Obsessing: How to Overcome Your Obsessions and Compulsions* (2001).

Specific phobia

Exposure to the feared object or event is the primary component of treatment for specific phobias. Both imaginal and *in vivo* exposure can be used effectively with or without relaxation training. Some specific fears do not interfere with usual activities and responsibilities and therefore it can be helpful to question whether the individual wishes to undertake treatment for this fear. It can also be helpful to question whether specific fears are out of proportion to the situation, as fear in some situations is appropriate, and learning to cope with these kinds of fears may be more helpful than attempting to eliminate them.

Social phobia (social anxiety disorder)

Exposure to feared situations is vital in treating social phobia. Exposure can be experienced through imaginal and *in vivo* situations and in role-playing activities within the session. It is important to assess the client's social and communication skills to plan appropriate social exposure tasks. If there are skills deficits, it may be useful to address this prior to exposure therapy. Learning relaxation exercises helps the client relieve anxiety symptoms; however, these may not be useful during exposure tasks depending upon the aims of the task. Cognitive strategies are also necessary both to challenge the client's perceptions that other people are making excessively negative judgements about them and to make them more resilient to such judgements. Assisting the client to tolerate some social disapproval, awkwardness, or embarrassment as an uncomfortable but normal, rather than disastrous experience, is also relevant.

The following describes a summary of strategies presented in this workbook that break the cycle of anxiety and panic as well as enhance well-being. This information is provided for clients in Handout 3.1.

- **Maintaining a healthy, balanced lifestyle**: Even though it is well docu-mented that lifestyle factors have an impact on emotional health, these aspects often are not thoroughly assessed in relation to stress and anxiety problems. Improvements in lifestyle factors alone can result in satisfy-ing changes for clients. Having a holistic view of mental health is vital to helping your clients reduce and manage stress and anxiety, as well as improving their resilience and reducing their vulnerability to stressors in the environment. Important aspects of a healthy life include getting enough sleep, eating well, exercising regularly, taking time out to relax or do something enjoyable, and effectively finding solutions to problems. The association between physical activity and psychological well-being has been established, and exercise has demonstrated benefits as a supplemen-tal or alternative treatment for depression, agoraphobia, panic disorder with agoraphobia, and generalised anxiety disorder (Burbach, 1997). Ways to maintain emotional health are further discussed in Chapter 4 with help-ful handouts on improving sleep, healthy eating, increasing physical and pleasurable activities, and problem solving.

- **Learning and practising relaxation and breathing techniques**: These tech-niques can help maintain a healthy outlook on life, reduce overall stress levels as well as help people to manage and cope with anxiety-provoking situations. The benefits of practising relaxation and breathing techniques and how to impart these skills to your clients are discussed further in Chapter 5. The attached CD provides much of this information in audio format along with a range of relaxation exercises to suit a variety of needs and preferences.

- **Identifying and modifying unhelpful thinking**: A prevailing and evi-dence-based notion derived from cognitive behavioural theory is that it is not a situation that causes stress, anxiety, or other unpleasant emotional states, but the interpretation of the event by the individual. Unhelpful thinking patterns and beliefs are thought to underlie emotional distur-bances including anxiety and depressive disorders. Becoming more aware of and then challenging and modifying unhelpful thoughts can help people alleviate and manage unpleasant emotional responses like anxiety, panic, guilt, and shame. Furthermore, the use of coping statements and affirmations can also be helpful both during and after anxiety-producing situations. Chapter 6 discusses how to identify and challenge unhelpful thinking patterns in more detail.

- **Stepping back and observing**: Sometimes people try to push their thoughts, unpleasant emotions, and physical symptoms away. However, fighting thoughts and feelings and trying to shut them out usually leads to more distress and frustration. Instead, when feeling uncomfortable, anxious, or distressed, it can be helpful and informative for people to take a step back and observe themselves experiencing their physical responses, emotions, and thoughts. Just noticing and observing without trying to change anything or to stop it in any way can be very therapeutic. Regularly practising this technique, called mindfulness, is likely to increase people's awareness of their thoughts and feelings and help them focus their mind more easily. This is described further in Chapter 6.

- **Facing fear**: Because the physical response to anxiety can be so unpleasant, uncomfortable, and scary, people often react by avoiding anything they think may cause heightened anxiety or a panic attack. Although avoiding can provide immediate relief, it is not a long-term solution and can actually increase and maintain fear and anxiety, as well as lead to isolation and depression. Taking small steps to face feared situations—graded exposure—assists people to realise that they can cope with discomfort, their anxiety eventually decreases when they stay in the situation, and their fear is often unfounded. This technique is sometimes paired with other behavioural and cognitive strategies (relaxation exercises, coping statements) to help manage anxiety symptoms during this process. Chapter 7 focuses on this technique and provides useful handouts to help your clients gradually overcome their fears.

- **Learning new skills**: Being able to problem-solve, make decisions, relate to and communicate with others, and to manage time effectively increases confidence in the ability to cope in a variety of situations, thereby reducing anxious feelings and avoidance behaviours. Skill-building is fundamental to cognitive behavioural therapy and is discussed throughout the book.

Strategies that enhance well-being and break the cycle of anxiety and panic

- **Maintaining a healthy, balanced lifestyle**: Lifestyle factors have an impact on emotional health and are vital to helping reduce and manage stress and anxiety as well as improving your resilience and reducing vulnerability to stressors in the environment. Important aspects of a healthy life include getting enough sleep, eating healthily, exercising regularly, taking time out to relax or do something enjoyable, and effectively finding solutions to problems.

- **Studying yourself**: Just the act of recording and monitoring thoughts, feelings, and behaviours has been shown to have therapeutic effects. For instance, research shows that writing down the experience of panic immediately after the experience of it can help people recover from panic disorder. A diary or thought record can also help bring clarity to the precipitants and maintaining factors of problem thoughts, feelings, and behaviours.

- **Learning and practising relaxation and breathing techniques**: These techniques can help maintain a healthy outlook on life and reduce overall stress levels as well as help you to manage and cope with anxiety-provoking situations. There are a range of relaxation exercises to suit a variety of needs and preferences.

- **Facing fear**: Because the physical response to anxiety can be so unpleasant, uncomfortable, and scary, people often react by avoiding anything they think may cause heightened anxiety, or a panic attack. Although avoidance can provide immediate relief, it is not a long-term solution and can actually increase and maintain fear and anxiety as well as lead to isolation and depression. Taking small steps to face feared situations assists you to realise that you can cope with discomfort, that your anxiety eventually decreases when you stay in the situation, and what you fear is probably not going to happen.

- **Identifying and modifying unhelpful thinking**: It is not necessarily a situation that causes stress, anxiety, or other unpleasant emotional states, but the interpretation by the individual of the event. Becoming more aware of and then challenging and modifying unhelpful thoughts can help you alleviate and manage unpleasant emotional responses like anxiety, panic, guilt, and shame. Furthermore, the use of coping statements and affirmations can also be helpful both during and after anxiety-producing situations.

- **Learning new skills**: Being able to problem-solve, make decisions, relate to and communicate with others, and manage time effectively increases your sense of confidence and ability to cope in a variety of situations thereby reducing anxious feelings and avoidance behaviours.

- **Stepping back and observing**: Sometimes people try to push their thoughts, unpleasant emotions, and physical symptoms away. However, fighting thoughts and feelings and trying to shut them out usually leads to more distress and frustration. Instead, when feeling uncomfortable, anxious, or distressed, it can be helpful and informative to take a step back and observe yourself experiencing physical responses, emotions, and thoughts. Just noticing and observing without trying to change anything or to stop it in any way can be very therapeutic. Practising this technique regularly is likely to increase your awareness of your thoughts and feelings and help you focus your mind more easily.

Chapter 4

Maintaining emotional health

This chapter focuses on fundamental lifestyle factors that when not adequately addressed can contribute to distress associated with stress and anxiety. The basic aspects of life like sleep, diet, exercise, pleasant activities, and physical health all need regular attention in order for an individual to have some resilience against everyday stress. When any one of these factors is not adequately attended to, people are more vulnerable to emotional stress.

The emotional health checklist is a useful and necessary tool to assist in assessing whether these basic needs are being met. Sometimes problems in these areas of functioning can indicate the degree to which stressors have impacted on an individual. Commencing interventions aimed at improving functioning in these areas is often of benefit during the assessment phase of therapy.

Lifestyle changes are not easy; therefore, the individual's interests, values, and attitudes should guide the planning so that they will be committed to the changes. Change should start from the baseline of the individual's current functioning and capacity and should occur in relatively small steps over a series of weeks or months. This is important in order to give the first planned changes the best chance of success, thereby motivating the individual to continue to make changes.

Consider that too few or too many activities and demands can lead both to stress and poor emotional functioning. Activity scheduling can be used to commence structured activities when there are too few activities. Time management skills can be used when there are too many demands and activities, and this includes making sure that some pleasant activities are a priority. Problem-solving can be helpful when unsustainable demands on a person are identified.

The planning of major life changes, such as moving house or changing jobs, should be considered in the context of an individual's emotional health. It may be that reviewing strategies to enhance emotional health and manage stress is a wise endeavour prior to planning these changes. If an individual is particularly vulnerable then it may be wise to postpone major life changes where possible.

If significant difficulties to do with lifestyle factors are identified, your client may require additional professional or practical assistance. Involve specialist professionals (dieticians, personal trainers, eating or sleep disorder clinicians) and inform your client about relevant services and resources in the community (sleep clinic, social clubs, housing, legal and financial assistance) as appropriate.

Emotional health check-up

Everyday lifestyle factors such as diet, exercise, sleep, general health, and use of drugs can contribute significantly to stress. A general check-up of these activities is an important place to start when attempting to reduce stress and anxiety and improve emotional health.

- **Diet:**
  Are you providing your body with the fuel it needs? Inadequate nutrients and energy will lead to physical and emotional stress. Are you eating the right kinds of foods? Are you eating them often enough?

- **Exercise:**
  Are you exercising enough? Exercise has been shown to improve mood and is also important for a regular sleep–wake cycle. A half hour of exercise three times a week that increases your heart rate is recommended to maintain physical and emotional health.

- **Sleep:**
  Do you have a regular sleep pattern? The amount of sleep required for each person varies but is commonly seven to nine hours. Frequent waking can also result in poor quality sleep.

- **Drug use:**
  Use of drugs can place your system under stress. Consider whether you may benefit from cutting down your use of drugs. Consider all drugs: caffeine (caffeinated soft drinks, coffee, chocolate, tea), alcohol, nicotine, over-the-counter medications, and other recreational drugs. The content of illicit drugs is not regulated so use of these drugs carries additional health risks as well as the risk of addiction.

- **Physical health:**
  Are you looking after any medical complaints, taking medication that is needed, or reviewing medication that you think might not be working well with your doctor? Do you have any persistent pain or worries about your physical health?

- **Practical concerns:**
  Do you have a satisfactory living situation? It is important to be able to count on having a safe and secure living environment where your basic needs are met. When accommodation or financial arrangements are inadequate additional support from community services may need to be sought.

- **Relationships and social support:**
  Do you have family or friends who support you and your goals? Social support enhances resilience and protects against mental health problems.

- **Pleasant activities:**
  Do you have activities that you enjoy doing every day? It can be easy to forget to make time for some simple, enjoyable activities, but this is necessary for emotional well-being.

Diet: fuel for a healthy mind

Review your diet according to the healthy eating pyramid below to consider where you need to make dietary changes. Also consider whether you consume any foods that you know from experience do not agree with you. If you think there may be substantial imbalances in your diet, it would be wise to keep a food diary rather than just relying on your memory of your diet.

If you are likely to need to make major changes to your diet or if you have a medical condition that places limitations on your diet, seek advice from a medical practitioner and/or dietician.

The healthy eating pyramid

(based on recommendations from the Harvard School of Public Health, 2007)

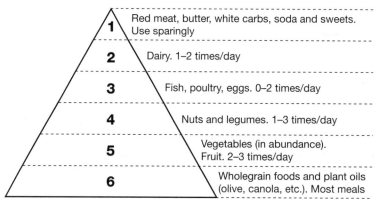

Source: <http://www.hsph.harvard.edu/nutritionsource/pyramids.html>

Planning changes in your diet

- **Ensure that appropriate food will be available.** Poor availability of appropriate food increases the likelihood that you will skip meals, become very hungry, and seek the easiest food option to satisfy your hunger—which is often food with poor nutritional value from vending machines and fast food outlets. Limiting the supply of unhealthy food at home, while ensuring a good supply of alternative healthy food options, is also likely to reduce consumption of it.

- **Eat regularly.** Stopping food intake for a long period of time will lead to cravings for fat and sugar, and slows down your metabolism.

- **Modify your existing diet.** Start with a small goal that you are likely to accomplish successfully. For example, if you are eating a lot of an unhealthy food try a gradual reduction in the amount or frequency. When you accomplish this you will feel motivated to cut down further. Do not cut out any food groups, including fats—all food is acceptable in moderation—and depriving yourself of certain foods can lead to binge-eating. Setting very large or extreme goals is unrealistic and counterproductive and is more likely to lead to failure, leaving you feeling defeated. On the other hand, making gradual progress by achieving smaller successes will serve to increase your motivation to achieve more.

- **Evaluate your success over a week**. You are likely to deviate from your eating plan from time to time; consider a setback as a normal aspect of the change process and then refocus on your goal. Do not use a scale to evaluate your success—you are aiming for a healthier lifestyle, not an "ideal" weight. Remember to acknowledge and reward your achievements.

- **Eat with awareness and enjoyment.** Plan to enjoy eating. Avoid eating while doing other activities so that you can appreciate your food, rather than eat it mindlessly. Look for healthy food options that you also find enjoyable. Notice the connection between hunger and eating, and how you feel after eating. You are likely to notice that eating is more satisfying when you are moderately hungry, when you consume nutritional food that you also enjoy, and when you eat a moderate portion of food.

- **Use alternative coping strategies.** Food may often be a comforting response to emotional states. This kind of eating is likely to be excessive and out of balance with your body's nutritional needs. If you notice that you are eating in order to cope with stress, boredom, or other emotions, plan to use alternative coping strategies (such as other pleasant or distracting activities) instead.

- **Seek professional medical advice when appropriate.** If you are substantially overweight or underweight then attending to your diet and exercise is an important health issue, and you are likely to benefit from support and advice from professionals such as medical practitioners and dietitians. Similarly, if an eating disorder is present, then assistance from a therapist experienced in this area is a priority.

Handout 4.2   Page 2 of 2

Treating Stress and Anxiety © 2008 Crown House Publishing and Dr Lillian Nejad and Katerina Volny

Exercise: the great mood enhancer

Information provided through public education campaigns has made it common knowledge that exercise is very important for long-term health and prevention of many common physical illnesses, such as cardiac disease. Perhaps not as widely known is that regular exercise can improve emotional health over a relatively short time frame.

It is recommended that people engage in some form of physical activity every day. More vigorous exercise that is associated with an increase in heart and breathing rate has been shown to be effective in improving mood.

Tips to start exercising

1. If you decide to take on a lot more exercise than usual, or if you have a medical condition, you should seek advice from a medical practitioner before commencing your new exercise schedule.

2. Plan your time to exercise, otherwise it may never happen. Consider it a priority. Fit exercise into your everyday routine, for example, walking to work or to the store or exercising on the way to or from daily chores.

3. Start slowly and increase gradually. If you are not exercising at all, then a five or ten-minute walk is a good start. When you can consistently do this first step without great exertion, lengthen the walk by five minutes or so. If you try to do too much too soon you are likely to find it to be difficult and perhaps even painful, making it a negative experience and leading to decreased motivation.

4. Choose physical activities that you enjoy, at least somewhat. Consider walking, tennis, swimming, golf, an exercise class, or team sports. Review your exercise regularly and change the activity if you get bored.

5. Having difficulty with motivation?
   - Plan to do an exercise class or exercise with a friend.
   - Consider all your reasons for exercising, for example, to feel better, look better, sleep better, health benefits, stronger or higher energy levels, better mood, less back pain or muscle tension.
   - Put your exercising shoes on and make a start. Once you start you may enjoy it more than you thought.

6. Make sure you warm up before and cool down after every session by doing gentle stretches.

7. Plan a contingency. If your exercise is dependent on another person, on having money, or on good weather, make sure you plan an alternative rather than not doing any exercise when obstacles arise. Plan an option for doing gentler exercise when feeling a little unwell. Also recognise that our physical condition varies from day to day, and you may perform better on some days than others.

Sleep well

How much sleep do you need?

Different people need different amounts of sleep. Adults average about 7.5 hours a night with a range from five to ten hours. There is no hard and fast rule about how many hours you should sleep. If you feel fine and rested after five hours of sleep, then you don't need more sleep. If you have five hours of sleep and you feel tired all the time, you may need more sleep.

How do you know if you have a sleeping problem?

Sleeping problems include not being able to fall asleep (for longer than thirty minutes), waking up very early in the morning and not being able to go back to sleep (total sleep less than six hours), and difficulty staying asleep during the night. If you are having one or more of these difficulties *and* you feel tired during the day, then you probably have a sleeping problem called insomnia. There are other kinds of sleeping problems, like nightmares, which can contribute to insomnia, while sleeping for too long can also make you feel tired during the day. This handout will mainly focus on insomnia.

How common are sleeping difficulties?

Most people experience problems sleeping once in a while. Up to 10% of people have chronic sleeping difficulties. So, if this is a problem for you, you are not alone!

You have a sleeping problem, what now?

The following pages describe "sleep well" strategies. Sleeping well depends on several factors: your *sleeping environment*, *breaking the stress–sleep cycle*, your *behaviour during the day*, and your *sleeping routine*. People have individual preferences; therefore, what works for someone else may not work for you. You may find that you only need one strategy to improve your sleep or that you need to implement several strategies over a period of time to see results. It is important to point out that if you have had long-term sleeping problems, you will probably need to use the following strategies for several weeks before you see any improvement.* Feeling tired during the day is often the last thing to improve. Both patience and persistence are keys to success.

---

* The strategies discussed are non-medical. If you would like information about sleeping medication, consult your medical practitioner.

Your sleeping environment

Many people do not realise how much their environment affects their ability to sleep.

The following are practical suggestions that you can implement immediately.

The ideal temperature

Generally, temperatures above 24 degrees and below 13 degrees centigrade will wake people. The ideal temperature range for sleep is from 17 to 20 degrees.

Fresh air

Some people prefer fresh air while they are sleeping.

Lights out

Light stimulates the brain to wakefulness, so you are more likely to sleep in a completely dark room. You may try heavy curtains or eyeshades to block out any unwanted light. If you feel uncomfortable with total darkness, a soft night light may be a useful alternative.

Turn down the volume

Noise levels affect sleep in various ways. If a noise is abrupt, unfamiliar, irregular, or intense, you are likely to have trouble sleeping. Some noises can help us to sleep—like "white noise", such as the sound of a fan or air conditioning. If you are unable to control unwanted noise in your environment, you may want to consider earplugs.

Sleeping with the enemy

Well, it can feel like they're the enemy if they are contributing to your sleeping problem! If you have different "sleep well" requirements than your partner, you are not alone. You may like to fall asleep to music while your partner prefers total silence. You may prefer fresh air, while you partner is unable to bear the breeze. You may like to read before bed, whereas you partner wants to sleep right away and needs total darkness. Or your partner snores. What's the answer? Well, there are two options, a new partner or some compromise! Since any partner is likely to cause some problems, compromise is the recommended strategy. Have a talk to your partner about your sleeping difficulties and come up with some practical ways to overcome your issues. Some helpful hints include: use eyeshades to cope with light, earplugs to cope with noise, agree to go to bed first so you can fall asleep before your partner starts snoring.

Bed matters

It makes sense to sleep on a surface that is comfortable and supports your back and neck properly. Clean and comfortable bedding is also likely to promote sleep.

Block clock

Hide your clock from view so you do not repeatedly check how long you have been unable to sleep and increase your stress about not sleeping.

Treating Stress and Anxiety © 2008 Crown House Publishing and Dr Lillian Nejad and Katerina Volny

The stress–sleep cycle

People often feel stressed when they find themselves unable to sleep. Unfortunately, the more stressed you become, the more likely you will not sleep well or at all. If you do not sleep well, you are likely to feel tired during the day which will make you less able to cope with stress. If you are less capable of managing stress, you are likely to increase your general stress levels which will make it even more difficult for you to sleep again. And so the problem continues until you learn to break the stress–sleep cycle by using the following strategies.

Don't lose sleep over it

Worrying about whether you will fall asleep or how tired you will be the next day is counterproductive. Your body will not be able to fall asleep if you are tense or worried. It may be helpful to know that if you lie relaxed in bed all night, it is almost as restorative as sleep. So, if you find yourself stressing about getting to sleep, refocus your thoughts. If you can change the way you think you can achieve a relaxed state, which will increase the likelihood that you will fall asleep. It can be helpful to tell yourself such things as, "I will just lie here and relax," "I will be able to cope tomorrow," "Even if I don't fall asleep, lying here in a relaxed state is the next best thing."

Worry well

Worrying is a part of life. So, if we are going to worry, we should do it well! Bedtime is not a good time to worry. The reason we do worry at bedtime is usually because we have been successful at distracting ourselves from our worries during the day by keeping busy with other things. You may feel okay during the day but at bedtime you suffer. Clearly, this is no way to live your life. Here's what you can do: set aside some time during the day to worry—you can call this "worry time". Choose a time every day that is convenient for you and pick a suitable amount of time to worry (half an hour or one hour). Use this time to think about your worries and about possible solutions. It can be helpful to write things down. It will take time to train yourself not to dwell on worries at other times of the day or night—*practice* is key here. What you can do if you worry outside of the organised time is to write the worry down and put it in a "worry box" (you can use an empty tissue box for this). Then, when it's your worry time, you can take your worries out of the box and deal with them appropriately. Keep the worry box beside your bed with a pen and a pad of paper for worries that come to you at night. This may seem like an odd suggestion, but if worrying is a major obstacle for you, it's worth a try.

Breathe and relax

Breathing and relaxation exercises can help you relax both your mind and body and assist in sleep. For more information about these techniques, refer to self-help books and CDs on relaxation and stress management that are widely available or consult a psychologist or counsellor. The internet also provides a wealth of information.

Behaviours during the day

You may be surprised to learn that what you do and don't do during the day can greatly influence sleeping patterns. Behaviours that interfere with sleep and behaviours that promote sleep are described below.

You snooze, you lose

Taking a nap may be tempting when you're tired, but if you are trying to sleep well at night, do not sleep during the day. Napping makes you feel less tired at night and causes your body to associate sleeping with the daytime rather than night time. If you feel as if you're falling asleep (like in front of the TV), change your activity.

Get physical

Physical activity is not only important for your health, but it also promotes sleep by lowering your general tension and stress that has built up during the day. The best time to exercise is late afternoon or early evening, about four to six hours before bedtime.

Watch what you eat, drink, and smoke …

Food, drink, and substances like cigarettes and diet pills have a stimulating effect on the body because they contain chemicals like tyrosine, caffeine, and nicotine. Tyrosine, contained in chocolate and cheddar cheese, can trigger heart palpitations; caffeine, contained in coffee, tea, chocolate, and fizzy drinks, can make it harder for you to fall asleep and stay asleep; and nicotine, the chemical in cigarettes, is an even stronger stimulant than caffeine. Many people use caffeine to help them stay awake during the day. Unfortunately, this just sets them up for another sleepless night. If you can't imagine your life without coffee, then make sure you have your last cup four to six hours before bedtime. If you don't want to quit smoking, have your last cigarette at least two hours before you go to bed. Diet pills and other drugs or drug interactions can also keep you awake. If you are taking any prescription or over-the-counter drugs, ask your doctor or pharmacist whether they can affect sleep.

Don't go hungry

It can be difficult to sleep if you are starving. If you need to eat something before bed, have a light snack like cereal or an apple (eating too much at night can also interfere with sleep). Try to avoid foods that cause gas (beans, peanuts, vegetables), are high in fat, or contain stimulants.

Don't drink and sleep

Many people use alcohol to fall asleep but it is not recommended. Too much alcohol at night often leads to problems staying asleep.

Keep a sleep diary

Gathering information about your sleeping habits will make you more aware of what is interfering with your sleep and what is promoting sleep (see last page of handout).

Handout 4.4 Page 4 of 5

Treating Stress and Anxiety © 2008 Crown House Publishing and Dr Lillian Nejad and Katerina Volny

Routine sleep

Having a routine is helpful in many areas of our lives, including sleep. A common sleeping routine is to change into your pyjamas, brush your teeth, set the alarm, and go to bed. Many people add other rituals before bed that help them to sleep well. The strategies below are suggestions that may work for you.

Get in the mood

Develop your own personal rituals before bed beyond the usual changing your clothes and brushing your teeth. Choose activities that help you relax and unwind like taking a bath, doing gentle stretches, listening to soothing music, or reading a book. When you decide what your routine will be, follow it every night so that it becomes a cue for your body to get in the mood for sleep.

Go to bed

Sleep only in your bed (not on the sofa) and use your bed only for sleeping and sexual activity. Don't use the bed or bedroom for work, studying, or watching TV unless it is a successful bedtime ritual.

Bedtime

Try to stick to a regular schedule for going to sleep and waking up, even at weekends and on holidays. However, if you feel sleepy at night, go to bed even if it's before your usual time. There is a natural sleep–wake cycle of about sixty to ninety minutes which means that if you feel sleepy but delay going to bed (to read one more chapter or to finish watching a TV show), you may not feel sleepy again for another hour and a half. So, if you feel sleepy, drop everything and go to bed. Make sure to wake up at the same time in the morning regardless of what time you go to bed.

Doze woes

If you go to bed and do not fall asleep within your usual time (generally fifteen to twenty minutes), get out of bed. *Trying* to sleep or worrying about not sleeping is counterproductive, so you are better off leaving the bedroom and doing something that is not too stimulating until you fall asleep. Some suggested activities are reading a boring magazine, practising a relaxation technique, or listening to soothing music. Only go back to bed when you feel sleepy. Repeat this every time you are unable to fall asleep. Remember to get up at the same time in the morning regardless of when you fall asleep.

Worth noting

- Sleeping too much or too little can be a sign of other problems like depression or physical ailments. If you experience sleeping difficulties and feel down or have changes in your appetite, consult your GP as soon as possible.
- If you want help in implementing these strategies ask your GP to refer you to a specialist.
- If you think you have a sleeping problem that is severely interfering in your quality of life, your GP can refer you to a sleep disorders clinic in your area.

Worksheet 4.1

Sleep diary

Here is an example of a sleep diary that can help you identify what "sleep well" strategies are working for you. Fill it in every day and, remember, it usually takes several weeks before you see improvement in your sleep. It can help to try just a few strategies at a time so you can determine what has been useful.

Date	Strategies used • sleeping environment • breaking the stress–sleep cycle • behaviours during the day • sleep routine	Time it took to fall asleep	Number of times awake	Total hours of sleep	Rate of tiredness during the day from 1 (not at all) to 10 (extremely)

Pleasant activities: a life worth living

Too many or too few activities and, in particular, too few pleasant activities, can increase and make you more vulnerable to stress and anxiety. If you find that you are not doing much during the day, writing a schedule or plan can help you increase your activities. If you can't fit in everything you want or need to do or you don't have enough time for sleeping, eating, physical activity, or for fun, then learning some time management skills or reviewing your priorities can help.

Pleasant activity suggestions

While the following list is by no means exhaustive, it can be used to stimulate ideas about pleasant activities. A wide range of pleasant activities needs to be considered to find the right balance of stay-at-home, social, active, relaxing, and stimulating pleasant activities for you.

- Cook something new
- Fix up something around the house
- Have a bath
- Do your nails
- Read a book, newspaper, or magazine
- Look up something on the internet
- Listen to music, and perhaps dance as well
- Play a musical instrument
- Have a conversation with family, a friend, or neighbour
- Watch a favourite TV show or movie
- Do a crossword or play a game
- Do some craft, drawing, painting, or writing
- Do some gardening
- Spend time with children or pets
- Go for a walk to a park or walk the dog
- Power-walk, jog, go to the gym, take a swim, or ride a bike
- Play a sport, such as tennis, netball, basketball, squash, or golf
- Do some yoga or stretching exercises
- Drive or take public transport to somewhere new
- Go out to see a movie, or go window-shopping
- Visit a friend
- Visit a gallery, museum, library, or market
- Start a short course or join a group or club
- Plan an outing or holiday
- Plan a dinner party or barbecue
- Buy something new
- Have a massage or haircut

Activity schedule

Choose activities that you like, are good at, fit with your long-term goals, and give you a sense of achievement. Use this worksheet to schedule activities or the following worksheet can be used to schedule at least one activity that is pleasurable and one that involves some physical activity per day.

Monday	AM	PM
Tuesday	AM	PM
Wednesday	AM	PM
Thursday	AM	PM
Friday	AM	PM
Saturday	AM	PM
Sunday	AM	PM

Time management

It is important to note that no matter how many things are on your "need to be done" list, the most efficient way of doing them is to do one thing at a time. It is also important to note that neglecting basic needs such as eating and sleeping is only likely to make stress and illness occur, and reduce your ability to complete your tasks. Use the following steps and the "To Do List" to assist you to do one thing at a time, starting with the most important task.

1. Write down everything that you have to do (divide big tasks into smaller tasks).

2. Estimate how much time each task will take—always overestimate to make room for interruptions or delays.

3. Add meal times and breaks (time to relax, have fun, physical activity, etc.) to your list of things to do. Consider a short break after every hour. If the task requires you to sit still, make sure you move around during your break.

4. Decide what are the most urgent priorities for the day and choose a reasonable number of tasks to accomplish given time estimates, meals, and breaks.

5. If you have an excessive number of tasks to complete for the time available, decide which tasks can be delegated or delayed.

6. Decide in what order you are going to accomplish your tasks. Some people like to get the most difficult task over with first and others like to start with easier tasks to gain momentum.

7. Do only one task at a time and finish what you start.

8. Review your progress and make adjustments to your list if necessary—DO NOT remove breaks and meals from your list.

9. Plan a reward for what you accomplish.

With practice, this will become a habit and you will become much more efficient and effective and much less stressed.

To do list

Priority rating	Tasks (include breaks and meals)	What order (1st, 2nd, 3rd)	Reward

Problem solving

1. What is the problem?

   Write down exactly your main problem or goal. Only address one problem at a time. You might find it helpful to discuss this with someone.

   Problem:

   _____

   _____

2. List all the possible solutions for the main problem.

   Write down all possible solutions, even ones that you are not keen on or that seem silly or unrealistic. Consider how other people may have addressed a similar problem.

   Brainstormed solutions:

   _____

   _____

3. Narrow down the list of solutions to the top three (or five) and list the pros and cons of each possible solution.

Solution	Pros	Cons

4. Choose the solution with the best benefits and that you have the resources to do now.

   Sometimes you may need to implement a temporary solution until you can get the resources to find a better, more permanent solution.

   Solution:

   _____

5. Plan how to carry out the best solution.

   List the obstacles:

   _____

   List resources required (include people who can help):

   _____

   Where can you access necessary resources?

   _____

   Write down the steps to carrying out your solution and a time schedule:

   Step 1 _____

   Step 2 _____

   Step 3 _____

6. Implement the solution

7. Review the solution
   Even if your plan did not produce a complete solution, notice now that you have more experience and information to plan and try another solution. Repeat the problem-solving process. Very difficult problems can require many attempts. Perseverance in overcoming obstacles is the key to success.

   Consider the following:
   • What did the solution achieve?
   • What did the solution fail to achieve?
   • What were the barriers when trying the solution?
   • Is the solution worth trying again with more help or better skills?
   • Is it worth trying a different solution?

Worksheet 4.4   Page 2 of 2

Treating Stress and Anxiety © 2008 Crown House Publishing and Dr Lillian Nejad and Katerina Volny

Social support

Stress and anxiety and other difficulties can lead to a breakdown in social contacts and isolation. Social support is an important factor for emotional well-being and an important resource for reducing, managing, and preventing stress and anxiety.

Reconnect with past positive relationships

Contact people with whom you have shared a positive friendship or shared interests.

Enhance current relationships

Reduce conflict and stress in current relationships by planning to do pleasant activities together.

- Plan to do activities that interest both people and are easy to do for both of you.
- Initially, do the activity for a relatively short time.
- Do the activity at a time that is convenient for you both.
- Try not to have specific expectations about how it will turn out—have an open mind. Be a scientist by treating this exercise as an experiment and see if it works.
- Avoid responding to or making harsh criticisms or put-downs.

Create opportunity to establish new positive relationships

This will require you to be in regular contact with groups of people. If you do not have this in your life currently it can be helpful to consider joining a low-key group that focuses on shared similar interests. This may be a support group, or a class that focuses on hobbies such as craft, exercise, or learning new skills. It is much easier to interact with other people when involved in an activity as you already have something in common.

Too shy?

Many people feel too shy to meet people or to socialise with others. Sometimes shyness can be due to not feeling confident with your social skills, like how to start or carry on conversations. The good news is that any skill can be learned. There are many self-help books on social and communication skills that can help. It can also be useful to learn the skills with a counsellor or therapist, individually or in a group.

Chapter 5

Relaxation and breathing exercises

Relaxation and breathing exercises have been shown to be effective stress management techniques and a component for treatment of anxiety disorders as well as other problems like insomnia and chronic pain. It is also worth noting that relaxation techniques have also been found to be effective in older populations (over 65 years of age) (Deberry, 1982; Rickard, Scogin & Keith, 1994; Scogin, Rickard, Keith & Wilson, 1992). Most relaxation techniques are based on the early work of Dr Edmond Jacobson's (1938) research on the benefits of progressive muscle relaxation. Relaxation exercises can provide relief in stress and anxiety-provoking situations as well as reduce overall levels of stress and anxiety. In addition to reducing the unpleasant physical symptoms of anxiety, relaxation exercises also affect cognitive processes—for instance, it can slow down racing thoughts, it can be a distraction for rumination, and it can help instil a sense of confidence and ability to cope in challenging situations.

As with learning any new skill, mastering relaxation techniques requires practice and this can not be emphasised enough. With practice, individuals become more aware and able to recognise the difference between a relaxed and a tense state, and take less and less time to foster a relaxation response. The aim of teaching these techniques is to enable clients to eventually produce a relaxed state within seconds. To produce the best results, clients should be instructed to practise relaxation exercises two times per day for one week and one time a day for four weeks thereafter and to practise short breathing exercises (thirty to ninety seconds) anytime they experience low levels of anxiety.

Teaching relaxation and breathing techniques can often be the best place to start in treating anxiety symptoms and disorders because it is regularly used in conjunction with other behavioural and cognitive techniques and it usually provides some symptom relief and distress reduction within a short period of time. This early success can improve people's motivation to try other behavioural or cognitive techniques that a clinician might suggest. Often, introducing clients to a brief deep abdominal breathing technique within the first session is very beneficial. It can be a powerful demonstration that they can quickly achieve a level of relaxation or stress/anxiety reduction by using a relatively simple skill; and more importantly, that change is possible, giving them an immediate sense of hope that is fundamental to the effectiveness of psychological treatment.

In some cases, relaxation will not be appropriate or the client's attitude towards relaxation is so averse that it is not worth starting with this technique. Some people experience a paradoxical effect when practising relaxation techniques in that they start to feel panicky or uncomfortable or fear that they will lose control. It is helpful to inform clients that sometimes this occurs and if they are feeling more anxious, they can discontinue the exercise. Furthermore, exercise caution when using relaxation exercises for individuals with psychotic disorders, particularly those who have auditory hallucinations, as they may confuse the relaxation script with their internal experiences.

If clients report that they have tried relaxation in the past and it wasn't effective, it can be helpful to further assess what techniques they practised and why they did not find it useful. Often clients have not been exposed to a variety of exercises and therefore have not found one that suits them best. Some may have experienced a paradoxical reaction and have catastrophised this event. Many have not been given an adequate rationale that helps them understand why relaxation techniques are beneficial. Others may not have practised the exercises sufficiently to observe any short or long-term benefits.

Anxious individuals, especially those with perfectionistic attitudes, will often worry whether they are doing it correctly and commonly believe that if they are distracted in any way then it's not going to work. Predicting and dispelling these beliefs before they start is very important. Furthermore, relaxation exercises can often assist people to fall asleep, and as insomnia is a common issue for people with stress or anxiety problems, using it for this purpose may be beneficial (but is separate from the above practice guidelines). Clients need to distinguish between using the techniques to learn to actively relax and using the techniques to fall asleep. In order to achieve a reduction in overall levels of stress and anxiety, as well as be able to better manage anxiety-provoking situations, practising the techniques without falling asleep is necessary.

The first step in relaxation training is explaining the rationale for practising relaxation and breathing techniques. Handout 1.3 describes the fight or flight response in anxiety and Handout 5.1 details the purpose of relaxation and can be given to clients to facilitate this education. Also, clients need to understand how to create the best conditions for learning relaxation including where and when to practise (see Handout 5.2) and they may be interested in the different techniques that are available to them (Handout 5.3). Handout 5.4 describes breathing techniques for clients who experience panic attacks. The CD *Relaxation Techniques: Reduce Stress and Anxiety and Enhance Well-Being* is especially designed to facilitate learning of relaxation and breathing techniques during and in-between therapy sessions, as well as to introduce them to a variety of exercises.

The purpose of relaxation exercises

Relaxation exercises have been shown to be effective stress management techniques and a component for treatment of anxiety disorders. The techniques are skills that require practice but once they are mastered, they can provide relief in stress and anxiety-provoking situations.

When a person is faced with a threat or worry, this triggers many physiological responses in the body including a release in adrenaline and an increase in heart rate. Our system works this way to provide energy for us to do something about the threat or worry. But if this occurs too often or too intensely, it can be uncomfortable, distressing, and even exacerbate health problems. Relaxation techniques assist the body to be in a relaxed rather than a stressed state, so our stress response occurs less intensely and less often.

Relaxation is incompatible with tension. You can't be both relaxed and tense at the same time. These techniques reduce the physical and cognitive symptoms associated with stress and anxiety like muscle tension and racing thoughts. It can also be used to reduce immediate and intense stress and anxiety as well as reduce your general overall stress and anxiety levels. Also, it increases your awareness of the feeling of relaxation and with practice it will take you less time to become relaxed.

Note: If anxiety is causing you significant distress and interruptions in your daily life, it is recommended that you seek individual psychological assistance.

Guidelines for relaxation

1. **Practice**: Try to have regular practice times every day. Research shows that practising relaxation twice a day for one week, and then once a day for four weeks thereafter is what is necessary to gain the benefits from this technique.

2. **Quiet place**: Find a place where you will not be disturbed or distracted.

3. **Be comfortable**: Lie down or sit down in a comfortable position and loosen your clothing.

4. **Don't stress about relaxation**: Just listen to the instructions and observe the results. There is no need to worry if you are "doing it right" or to judge yourself or your ability to perform the relaxation exercise. It's normal to be distracted by external (traffic, people talking) or internal (your thoughts, bodily noises) activity. In fact, one of the benefits of relaxation is that it makes you more aware of your own thoughts. Part of the practice of relaxation is to notice that you are distracted and direct yourself back to attending to the exercise.

5. **Don't fall asleep**: The purpose of practising relaxation is to learn to *actively* relax. Sleeping is a passive form of relaxation. You may use relaxation for sleep if you like (especially if you are having trouble sleeping); however, this is not considered practising relaxation for the purpose of reducing overall stress levels and anxiety.

6. **Try several forms of relaxation**: People have individual preferences, and relaxation exercises are no exception. There are a wide variety of relaxation exercises and you may want to try several versions to find the best fit for you. You may also find that you like to do a variety of relaxation exercises for different purposes or to prevent monotony.

Types of relaxation exercises

There are a range of relaxation techniques that suit each individual's specific needs and preferences. The following describes six types of exercises that help manage and reduce stress and anxiety as well as enhance well-being. These exercises are available on CD: *Relaxation: Techniques to Reduce Stress and Anxiety* (Nejad & Volny, 2007).

- **Abdominal breathing**: When people are stressed or anxious, they usually take shallow, quick breaths that can lead to uncomfortable and sometimes scary physical responses. Abdominal breathing is the opposite of this; it involves slow, deep breaths all the way down into your abdomen and then exhaling completely. This triggers a relaxation response. Abdominal breathing is a handy skill to learn because you can use it anywhere without others noticing. It's useful to learn this skill before the other relaxation exercises because most of them include abdominal breathing. When you have mastered this technique, you can use it when you feel tense or worried or when you are about to face a difficult or challenging situation.

- **Progressive muscle relaxation**: This exercise was developed by Dr Edmund Jacobson in 1938. It involves tensing different muscles for up to fifteen seconds and then relaxing them to create a deep state of relaxation. It is important to put effort into tensing each muscle without overexerting yourself; however, if tensing the muscle is causing you any pain or if you have an injury, do not tense this muscle group. Instead, focus on relaxing the muscle and then move on to the next one. If you have trouble holding the tension in the time allotted, simply hold it for as long as seems right for you. In addition to reducing stress and anxiety, progressive muscle relaxation has been shown to be effective in reducing insomnia and chronic pain.

- **Visualisation**: To reduce anxiety, fear, or tension it can be helpful to retreat to a safe or calming place. Because it is not always possible or practical to actually go to a real setting where you feel safe and at peace it can be useful to visualise a scene in your mind. Where would you go if you could when you feel stressed or anxious? What is the first place that pops in your mind? It may be a specific location that actually exists like a room in your house, a warm bath, or a bench in a nearby park. It may be a particular landscape that you find soothing or relaxing like a beach, forest, or mountaintop. Or it may be an invention of your imagination such as a place in outer space or in a bubble. It's your choice. When you visualise your safe place, make it an experience that all your senses can enjoy. Note the unique features of your setting: the colour, the smells, the temperature, and the textures—the more details, the better. It may be difficult to think of a place that will be helpful for you. You may find that several scenes are soothing or that you may use different settings for different situations. Visualisation exercises can be a guide to creating your own safe place or it can help construct a specific scene for you. Keep in mind that this technique is not meant to be used as an avoidance strategy. Sometimes avoiding certain situations and places is warranted; however, relaxation exercises are designed to equip you to face anxiety-provoking or feared situations, not to help you avoid them. If you are not sure that you can distinguish between situations that should be avoided or need to be confronted, seek the opinions of trusted members of your family, friends, or a health professional.

- **Relaxation exercise for coping**: When experiencing anxiety, it is common to have thoughts that something terrible will happen. These thoughts are often unrealistic and lead to an increase in our distress. If we notice these thoughts and replace them with more realistic thoughts, we can relieve anxiety. Often people think that the experience of anxiety is a sign that they are going crazy, having a physical collapse, or losing control of themselves. It is important to know that anxiety by itself does not cause sudden physical damage, it does not cause people to become crazy, or to lose control of their mind or actions.* Relaxation exercises can help you challenge your unhelpful thoughts to enable you to effectively cope with anxiety, worry, and fear.

- **Activity-based relaxation exercises**: It can be helpful to practise relaxation exercises while doing an activity like walking. More active relaxation exercises are designed to assist you to focus your attention on one task while in conjunction with deep abdominal breathing. When trying to focus our attention, it is common for our mind to wander frequently onto many other topics. We can become more skilled at focusing our attention by noticing when our mind wanders and reminding ourselves to focus our attention to the task at hand. We might have to do this several times in a few minutes.

- **Brief relaxation**: As you become more proficient at using the relaxation techniques, you will find it easier to relax using brief exercises. It is useful to develop your own brief relaxation technique that you can use anytime and anywhere when a stressful situation may arise. Start by noticing your breath and commencing abdominal breathing in a comfortable rhythm. Then you can add your own personal touch that may involve relaxing particular muscle groups, visualising soothing images, or reminding yourself of helpful self-statements. You could imagine yourself dealing with this situation well, or tell yourself that you have survived difficult situations before, or just observe your anxiety and stress coming and going like a wave. Use the cues and strategies for relaxation that work best for you.

---

* If you are experiencing anxiety symptoms for the first time, it is recommended that you see your doctor for a medical check-up to rule out any physical causes for your symptoms.

Handout 5.3   Page 2 of 2

Breathing during a panic attack

Panic attacks involve the sudden onset of intense and uncomfortable physical symptoms like hyperventilation, heart palpitations, dizziness, blurred vision, tingling sensations in the hands and feet, chest pain, a choking sensation, nausea, stomach pain, shaking, and sweating. These symptoms can be so strong that it is not uncommon for people to think that they are having a heart attack or going crazy.

Although the way our bodies respond during a panic attack can be very frightening and distressing, they are not harmful.* In fact, this response serves a protective function when we are under threat.

One of the most common sensations in the early stages of anxiety and panic is feeling short of breath. When people feel short of breath, their natural response is to try to take in more oxygen; however, this actually exacerbates the symptoms. Overbreathing or hyperventilation leads to a decrease in carbon dioxide in your body and generates a chain of physiological events that lead to the panic symptoms described above.

You can reverse this pattern by learning to breathe differently in this situation:

1. Inhale carbon dioxide by cupping your hands over your mouth and breathing in and out. You can also use a paper bag.

2. Even though you feel like you need to inhale deeply, being short of breath is an indication that you are not exhaling properly. You need to exhale all the way.

If you use these two breathing tips, you will be able to prevent full-blown panic attacks and/or reduce the duration and intensity of the symptoms. Remember, it is also very helpful to think differently about your symptoms; accept them rather than fight them, understand them rather than be frightened of them. A therapist can help you to learn and practise these techniques.

---

*If you have experienced panic symptoms for the first time, it is recommended that you see your doctor for a medical check-up to rule out any physical causes for your symptoms.

Chapter 6

The impact of thoughts on stress and anxiety

This chapter describes strategies to help clients identify, challenge, and modify unhelpful thought patterns in order to both reduce anxiety and reduce the impact of anxiety. Therapists will have already commenced some cognitive techniques from the beginning of the therapeutic process by offering education that modifies the client's understanding of their experiences and attitudes towards treatment. For example, identifying and challenging clients' unhelpful or unrealistic thoughts about their presenting issues, about their ability to change, and about psychological therapy is an important part of engaging them and reducing their anxiety associated with therapy. This process can serve as an example of how modifying cognitions can reduce anxiety and produce change.

The classic form of cognitive therapy is based on the theory that all emotions are preceded by thoughts, and therefore modifying problematic thoughts can relieve distress. It is necessary to orient clients to the process and rationale for cognitive therapy, and the relationship of cognitions to emotions and behaviours (see Handout 6.1). This is followed by psychoeducation about common unhelpful thoughts (Handout 6.2). It is important to both normalise these thought patterns as well as acknowledge the need to change these patterns if they are causing significant distress or disruption to one's life.

Self-monitoring unhelpful thoughts and recording thoughts, emotions, and behaviours associated with distressing situations are the next steps (Worksheet 6.1). This assists clients to identify the primary unhelpful thought patterns. Clients greatly benefit from the input and analysis of thought patterns from the therapist, as they are often unaware of their problematic thoughts or may identify thoughts that may not be at the core of their anxiety. Once the primary thoughts that require modification are identified, the therapist assists the client to challenge their thoughts by questioning their validity, asking them to gather evidence to support or dispel their beliefs, and by helping them to adjust their thoughts to ones that are more adaptive or realistic (Worksheet 6.2). Sometimes the target for modification is not the content of the thoughts, but rather the thought pattern itself, i.e., excessive worrying, rumination, or obsessive thinking. Handout 6.3 describes ways of managing these sorts of thought patterns.

We have also included additional strategies to help manage distressing thoughts because an individual's capacity and keenness to undertake cognitive therapy can vary. Furthermore, during especially difficult times in life, an individual may require a variety of strategies to cope effectively. These additional strategies include those that are influenced by Eastern meditation and mindfulness techniques which are accumulating evidence-based support for the treatment of a variety of disorders and difficulties.

Mindfulness is an ancient practice found in Eastern philosophies, including Buddhism. It has been adapted and incorporated into therapies that have been found to effectively treat borderline personality disorder, chronic pain, stress, anxiety, depressive relapse, and disordered eating (Baer, 2003; Linehan, 1993; Brantley & Kabat-Zinn, 2003; Kabat-Zinn, 1990; Segal, Williams & Teasdale, 2002). Mindfulness involves bringing attention or awareness to the present moment in a non-judgemental manner. Being mindful is about just noticing and observing, without trying to change anything or to stop or prolong the experience in any way. It can be applied to any situation, from doing the dishes to tasting chocolate to smelling a rose. For example, walking mindfully entails absorbing yourself in the experience by attending to the particular sensations and experiences of walking. Of course, the mind naturally wanders and it is important not to try to block out these thoughts. In fact, becoming distracted by thoughts (of what you need to do today, about past events or experiences, or hopes or fears of the future) is a normal part of the process of mindfulness. The practice of mindfulness is to notice that one's mind has wandered and then redirect your attention back to the present moment. Mindfulness practices can assist people to experience and cope with painful emotions, to increase awareness of avoidance behaviours, to become less judgemental about the self, others, and life in general, and to participate in the experience of everyday activities. Mindfulness can also enhance the practice of relaxation activities as it can help individuals to redirect their attention and to participate more fully in the exercise (see Handouts 6.4 and 6.5).

Thoughts, emotions, and behaviour: how they work together

In order to manage stress and anxiety effectively, we need to understand all the components of this experience. Just like links in a chain, each of the following events make up our experience:

Situation
↓
Thoughts and images
↓↑
Physical response
↓↑
Emotional response
↓↑
Behaviour

Stressful situations

Specific situations, such as events where there is some risk of failure, harm, or criticism from others, may be the trigger that sets off a series of reactions leading to stress and anxiety. For example, the anticipation of an important performance, test, or task, may trigger stressful thoughts. Facing people with whom you have uneasy or unpleasant relationships, and facing an activity that was associated with a bad experience, such as returning to driving after a car accident, may also be triggers to a stressful response.

Several small stressors can also accumulate to cause problems. It is important to consider that more general sources of stress may cause greater vulnerability to stress and anxiety. Circumstances such as lack of sleep, illness, or having an argument with someone may make it more likely for stress and anxiety to be triggered. It can often be the case that events that we normally cope with cause a severe stress reaction at times when we are rundown.

Thoughts

Our response to any situation depends on the kind of thoughts we have about that situation. This explains why one person can enjoy an event and another person can't stand it or can't cope. For example, speaking to a group of people is something that many would find daunting, while others would relish the challenge. These responses are often shaped by previous experiences. A person that is practised in public speaking and has had many good experiences in the past might be thinking about how they are looking forward to impressing others and being the centre of attention. A person that has done very little of this, or had a very negative

Handout 6.1   Page 1 of 3

experience in the past, might be anticipating possible failure, such as forgetting what to say, shaking or stuttering, and other people thinking poorly of them. This demonstrates how emotions like fear or enthusiasm are preceded by thoughts. This also means that if we have thoughts that lead to distressing emotions, if we modify or change the thoughts, we can modify or change the distressing emotions.

Identifying thoughts can be difficult because sometimes they occur automatically without us even being aware of them. Use the worksheets to record your thoughts at the time of feeling difficult emotions. The more you do this, the more aware of your thoughts you will become. If you are having difficulty, review the following questions to help uncover the relevant thoughts.

- Are you thinking of a negative outcome that could happen in the future?
- Are you thinking of a bad experience in the past?
- Are you thinking about not achieving your goals?
- Are you thinking of how others might see you?

Physical and emotional response

Physical and emotional responses are the parts of our experience that cause us distress and pain. Some people may be better at recognising either the physical or the emotional part of their experience rather than noticing their thoughts.

Common physical manifestations of stress and anxiety are headaches, muscle tension, stomach discomfort, nausea, indigestion, feeling hot and sweaty, heart pounding, shortness of breath, and shaking.

Stress and anxiety are associated with a broad range of emotions. If you haven't been used to describing your emotions it may be difficult at first. If you are having difficulty describing a feeling select the few feelings that seem to fit best at the time. See Handouts 1.2 and 1.4 which list physical and emotional responses to stress and anxiety.

Behavioural response

Our behavioural response is what we do to cope with a stressful experience. Reflecting on these behaviours can assist us to identify our positive and negative responses and coping patterns, and help us plan to use more helpful and effective strategies in the future.

There are a wide range of options for coping with stressful experiences. For example, when feeling anxious about going to an event, common responses might be to grit your teeth, remind yourself of why the event is important, go and face the fear, confide in a friend who will provide moral support and encouragement, start drinking wine as soon as you get there, or just stay at home and watch TV. See Handouts 1.2 and 1.4 for a list of common behavioural responses to stress and anxiety.

Handout 6.1   Page 2 of 3

Recording your patterns of triggers, thoughts, and emotions

Get to know your personal pattern of physical and emotional responses by recording them as they occur. Just recording the thoughts, feelings, physical responses, and behaviours associated with anxiety-provoking or stress-inducing situations is therapeutic in itself. It is an important part of managing stress and anxiety because it raises awareness about thought patterns and at the same time it reduces stress and anxiety levels.

Often emotional distress is the first thing that we notice about stress and anxiety; therefore, you may find it easiest to record how you feel first and then work back to the situation and thoughts that preceded the distress. Once you have recorded the situation, thoughts, physical responses, emotions, and behaviours, rate your level of distress on a scale of 0 to 100, where 0 is no distress, and 100 is the most severe distress imaginable. Your rating will give you an idea of where to start in terms of modifying thoughts and behaviours. Some people like to work on areas that cause the most distress while others like to start with something that causes less distress and work up to situations that cause the most distress. Both strategies have their benefits and it is helpful to talk through with your therapist what approach will best meet your needs.

Handout 6.1   Page 3 of 3

Detecting unhelpful thoughts

Getting to know your patterns of stress and anxiety is an important step in improving your management of them. Keep a record of times that you experience noticeable stress or anxiety. As you do this regularly, you will become more aware of the components of your experience of stress and anxiety.

Situation (triggers and vulnerabilities)	Thoughts and images	Physical feelings	Emotional feelings	Distress rating	Behaviour

Challenging unhelpful thoughts

Everyone has unhelpful and unrealistic thoughts that can lead to intense and unpleasant emotions. Reviewing whether or not the thought is realistic or helpful and in turn making adjustments to your thoughts is an effective way of reducing emotional distress. The following describes ways in which thoughts can be unhelpful and offers suggestions for readjusting them.

Common examples of unhelpful thinking

Anticipating disaster

You may find yourself predicting that a future negative event will occur without considering how likely this may be and disregarding the alternative positive or neutral outcomes that might occur.

Perfectionistic thinking

You may find yourself thinking that if you don't complete a task perfectly, you have failed or you will fail to achieve future goals. Because of these unrealistic expectations, you commonly think of yourself as a failure and often feel hopeless or frustrated. Striving for perfection is counterproductive as, in reality, people do not perform perfectly and need to make mistakes to learn.

Global thinking

If you often use words like *always* or *never*, *all* or *nothing*, *everything* or *nothing*, *everyone* or *no one*, you are likely to have a global style of thinking. This means that instead of describing and interpreting situations and events in a specific and realistic way, you tend to overgeneralise, exaggerate, and/or catastrophise the event and the impact of the event.

Minimising strengths, maximising weaknesses

You may pay more attention to your flaws and limitations—and ignore your assets and strengths—giving you a distorted, unbalanced view of yourself. Everyone has both strengths and weaknesses. Acknowledge those qualities that have helped you through difficult situations in the past, the attributes that other people admire, and the characteristics that make you unique.

Worrying about what others think

You may be overly concerned about how others perceive you or how others may react to your wants, needs, or behaviours. This can make you feel the need to please others all the time so they like you or it may make you too anxious to be around people. It is unlikely that others are as critical of you as you think; they are most likely more preoccupied with their own concerns and worries. However, if people are critical of you, that's also not the end of the world. It's important to decipher constructive criticism from damaging remarks and to learn how to respond effectively to both circumstances.

Handout 6.2   Page 1 of 2

Treating Stress and Anxiety © 2008 Crown House Publishing and Dr Lillian Nejad and Katerina Volny

Believing all your thoughts are true

Unhelpful, unrealistic, and anxiety-provoking thoughts are often related to messages and values learned during childhood, and therefore, were never questioned or challenged. These thoughts are often attached to strong feelings and memories making them seem true, valid, and indisputable. As an adult, it is important that you give yourself the opportunity to question and dispute these thoughts and beliefs using your life experience, knowledge, and common sense as a guide to developing your own value system.

Here are some questions you can ask yourself regarding your thoughts and beliefs:

- Is there any evidence to suggest that your anxiety-provoking thought might be inaccurate or exaggerated?
- Have you experienced similar situations before and performed reasonably well?
- Even if things don't go well, is it likely that you could cope with it or get assistance or support?
- Are you dwelling on thoughts of negative experiences from the past without also remembering positive experiences from the past?
- Are you worrying about possible negative events in the future that you can't possibly predict or prepare for now? Are you considering all the positive events that could happen in the future?
- Check the words that you are using for your anxiety-provoking thought. Are you thinking that you will *always* have a particular problem, or that you will *never* achieve a goal? Is this thinking out of proportion and unrealistic? Have you some of the time, or even most of the time, been able to get by without substantial problems? What goals have you achieved?
- Where did your thought or belief come from? Does it make sense to you? Does it help you achieve your goals in life? Does it make you feel good or bad about yourself? Is it time to question this thought or belief?

Examples of more helpful thoughts

The following are some common examples of more helpful thoughts. When you have come up with alternative thoughts that are right for you, try writing them on a card and keeping them with you. Use the card to remind you regularly of your new thoughts and to apply them in anxiety-provoking situations.

"Most times I have been in this kind of situation I have done reasonably well, so I'll probably do well this time too."

"Even if things don't go as I would prefer I can probably cope. I could get some help to look at my other options."

"Even if I do get panicky or anxious, I can take a break, concentrate on my breathing, and remind myself that this feeling doesn't last for very long."

"People have their own lives to lead; they probably don't have time or don't care to notice my imperfections. Even if they do, so what?"

Handout 6.2   Page 2 of 2

Transforming your unhelpful thoughts into helpful thoughts

By completing this worksheet regularly you will practise replacing unhelpful thoughts with helpful thoughts, reduce your emotional distress, and develop healthier thinking habits.

Situation	Thoughts	Emotion	Distress rating	More helpful/realistic thought	New distress rating

Tips to manage worrying

Worrying is a natural part of our thinking process. However, some people spend all their time worrying about everything, major and minor, and this can cause significant problems in their daily life, in their relationships, and in how they experience different situations. Excessive worrying can lead to avoiding or not being able to fully enjoy various events and situations, not being able to make even the simplest decision, and feeling physically tense and uneasy most of the time. Stress from prolonged worrying can lead to more serious physical and emotional problems. Therefore excessive worrying can actually lead to something to worry about!

The following tips can help you to break this cycle (it can be helpful to work through these strategies with a trained therapist):

- Learn a variety of relaxation and breathing strategies. This can help you reduce your overall levels of stress and help you face anxiety-provoking situations. It can also help distract you from your worries. Use a CD or tape to guide you through the exercises.

- It is important to learn how to distinguish between worries that require your attention and worries that are unnecessary. The following questions can help you clarify this:

    "Can I do something about this problem?"
    "Is this something I always worry about, but nothing ever happens?"
    "Is this something that has a solution?"
    "Will my worrying make this situation better or worse or have no effect at all?"

- If there is something you can do about the problem, take action. People often delay or avoid taking action or making decisions because they are worried about making a mistake. Unfortunately we can't predict the future, so in every decision we make there is a chance that it may or may not go well. The important thing to remember is that whatever happens you will be able to deal with it. The only way to decrease worry about making mistakes is to learn that you can cope with making mistakes. Set a time limit for making a decision, write down your reasons for making the decision, and then follow through. Keeping a decision-making diary (similar to the worry diary described below) can help during this process.

- If there is nothing you can do and worrying does not make the situation better, tell yourself that your worries are not helpful and let them go. It can help to challenge your thoughts about the worry and ask yourself, "Where's the evidence for that?" or "What would be so bad about that?" or "Is this problem so important that I should spend all my time thinking about it?" Relaxation, breathing, distraction, and just observing your thoughts come and go can also help reduce your worrying.

- Study your worries by keeping a worry diary. Write down what you fear might happen (be as specific as possible) and then later write down if what you were worried about actually happened, whether it was as bad as you expected, and what you did to cope with the situation. This will help you understand your worries better, distinguish between worries that are useful and those that are useless, and help you realise that you can cope no matter what happens.

- Set aside some time during the day to worry—you can call this "worry time". Select a time every day that is convenient for you and pick a suitable amount of time to worry (half an hour, one hour). Use this time to think about your worries and about possible solutions. It can be helpful to write things down. It will take time to train yourself not to dwell on worries at other times of the day or night. *Practice* is key here. What you can do if you worry outside of the organised time is to write the worry down and put it in a "worry box" (you can use an empty tissue box for this). Then, when it's your worry time, you can take your worries out of the box and deal with them appropriately. Keep the worry box beside your bed with a pen and a pad of paper for worries that come to you at night. This may seem like an odd suggestion, but if worrying is a major problem for you, it's worth a try.

- Create "worry-free zones" or places where you have decided that you are not to worry. You can start with one zone, like a room in your house, and expand these zones over time as you gain more control over your worries. If you find yourself worrying in a worry-free zone, just notice it and let it go, or try to delay it until you are not in the zone.

- You may have found that worrying has prevented you from enjoying or doing things that you used to value. Start scheduling in pleasant activities to enrich your life.

- It can help to imagine a situation that is worrying you and then imagine yourself being able to cope well in the situation. Pay attention to how you feel when you successfully cope in a situation.

Handout 6.3   Page 2 of 2

More strategies to manage persistent unhelpful thoughts

Ideally you will be able to identify and dispute unhelpful, unrealistic, and anxiety-provoking thoughts and change them to more helpful and realistic thoughts. This "cognitive therapy" strategy is a good option because as your thinking habits become healthier, a major source of distress will be removed from your life. However, there are several more very helpful techniques to manage thoughts that lead to distress. These strategies may be useful at particularly difficult times in life when you are feeling overwhelmed with stress.

Distraction

If you have noticed that you are preoccupied with persistent, worrying thoughts, distraction can be a powerful tool to bring relief. Ideally your distracting activity will be something that is relatively familiar, pleasant, and that absorbs your attention. Either more mentally active or more physically active distracting activities may suit you best. It is useful if you choose your distraction techniques before you have the symptoms because it is difficult to try to think of what to do when the symptoms have already started. Make a list of distracting activities and put it somewhere visible so that next time you are feeling stuck with distress you can use this list.

Suggestions include: read a good book, play with a pet or child, watch something you like on TV, do some household chores or work that you enjoy, go for a walk, take a bath, listen to music that usually puts you in a positive or relaxed mood, make a phone call to a good friend, do some kind of craft work or gardening, count backwards from 100, say the alphabet backwards, look at the pictures in a magazine, focus on describing something in the room, sing to music, or talk to someone.

Distraction may not always be as simple as it sounds. Even though you may carry out a distracting activity your stress-provoking thoughts are likely to return and interrupt you. This is to be expected especially if worrying has been a long-standing pattern of thinking. When it does happen, just notice it without judging yourself and then turn your attention back to your task. For example, if you are out walking and you begin to worry again, just notice that you have started to worry again and then remind yourself to enjoy the view, or if you are cooking remind yourself of the next step in the recipe.

It is important to note that although distraction is very effective, the old adage "you can never get enough of a good thing" does not apply. Always avoiding situations and distracting yourself from your feelings is not healthy and can lead to increased anxiety and fear. So, use distraction in moderation.

Letting go

Our mind works so that once we think of one stress or anxiety-inducing problem, we are likely to think of other similar problems in life that have occurred in the past or could happen in the future. Letting go rather than dwelling on stressful thoughts is a skill. With practice we can become better at this. The process of letting go involves first noticing the thought, then describing it in an objective and non-judgemental way, and finally allowing the thought to pass. It can be helpful to imagine the thought passing like clouds floating by in the sky, a balloon flying through the air, or waves lapping on a beach.

For example, when giving a talk at an important public event, negative thoughts may come to mind. Dwelling on these thoughts would increase anxiety, so instead:

Just notice: "There's that thought again that I might stutter and forget my speech."

Describe: "This thought is unhelpful and makes me feel anxious" or "My hands are sweaty."

Let go: "The thought will just come and go—it's just passing through my mind."

Being mindful

Mindfulness is an ancient practice found in Eastern philosophies, including Buddhism. Mindfulness involves bringing attention or awareness to the present moment in a non-judgemental manner. Being mindful is about just noticing and observing, without trying to change anything or to stop or prolong the experience in any way. It can be applied to any situation from doing the dishes to tasting chocolate to smelling a rose.

For example, walking mindfully entails absorbing yourself in the experience by attending to the particular sensations and experiences of walking (how your limbs move, the feel of the ground on your feet, your breathing rate increasing as you walk faster, the wind on your face, etc.). Of course, the mind naturally wanders and it is important not to berate yourself for becoming distracted or to try to block out these thoughts. In fact, becoming distracted by thoughts (of what you need to do today, about past events or experiences, or hopes or fears of the future) is a normal part of the process of mindfulness. The practice of mindfulness is to notice that your mind has wandered and then redirect your attention back to the present moment.

Mindfulness practices can assist people to experience and cope with painful emotions, to increase awareness of avoidance behaviours, to become less judgemental about the self, others, and life in general, and to participate in the experience of everyday activities.

Handout 6.4   Page 2 of 4

Suggestions for mindfulness activities

- **Notice your breath:** Slowly breathe in and out; notice how the air feels in your nostrils as you breathe in, notice the time it takes between inhaling and exhaling, and how it feels to breathe out through your mouth. Remember that becoming distracted is normal; if this happens, just notice the thought passing through your mind, and redirect your attention to your breath.

- **Tasting chocolate:** Feel the texture of the chocolate on your tongue and how it changes as it melts in your mouth—notice how you naturally will either suck on it or chew it. Taste the chocolate without any judgement, good or bad. After you swallow it, notice the taste left in your mouth. Do not try to prolong the sensation in any way, just notice it.

- **Doing the dishes:** Observe yourself picking up items in the sink, the texture of the object in your hands, how your hands feel under warm water, the feel of soap and water as you clean the dish or cup. Notice the changes in water temperature and pressure as you do the dishes. Observe how you place the object in the dishwasher or tray.

Accepting

Accepting thoughts

When experiencing distress, "accepting" is usually the last thing we want to do. Instead we might be thinking that it is very unfair to be experiencing distress and that we would do anything to get away from it. This kind of thinking can actually cause more pain and distress. Trying to push away the reality of something that we can't change generates frustration, makes the emotion stronger, and is counterproductive. Accepting doesn't mean saying that it's okay or fair to be in a distressing situation, it just means acknowledging the situation in a realistic manner.

Frustration-inducing thoughts	Accepting and coping thoughts
"This shouldn't be happening."	"This situation is unpleasant and unfair."
"I can't stand it."	"I don't like this but I can cope and get through this."

Accepting emotions

Accepting the experience of distressing emotions is also an important skill to have in order to have a healthy and functional emotional system. Expecting that you should always be able to cope in life without experiencing significant distress is unhelpful and unrealistic. Another unhelpful assumption is the belief that if most people don't publicly show distress, they don't experience it. These expectations and assumptions can lead individuals to think they are bad or faulty just for experiencing distressing emotions, making them feel isolated and alone, which generates

Handout 6.4   Page 3 of 4

Treating Stress and Anxiety © 2008 Crown House Publishing and Dr Lillian Nejad and Katerina Volny

further distress. We can relieve some of our suffering if we acknowledge and accept that distressing experiences and emotions are part of life. Accepting yourself and your responses rather than judging yourself will enable you to acknowledge your emotions as well as manage them more successfully.

Accepting others' responses

Sometimes other people will convey ideas that the emotions you experience are excessive or wrong, and can give advice such as, "Just pull yourself together," or "Forget about your emotions and get on with it." These kinds of messages usually make people feel even worse, often leading to anger towards others or guilt and shame for not being able to cope. Clearly this is unhelpful. However, we cannot control what others say or think; we only have power over our own responses. Therefore, it can be helpful to expect and accept that others may make unhelpful or judgemental comments and plan how you will deal with the situation. For example, let the person know what they could do to help you, walk away and tell yourself that it is okay to feel anxious sometimes, and try to steer clear of people who make unhelpful comments.

Affirmations

These are positive statements that you say to yourself to replace negative thoughts or worries. Examples of affirmations are:

- "I accept the natural ups and downs of life."
- "It's never too late to change. I am improving one step at a time."
- "I love and accept myself the way I am."

In order for affirmations to help, you have to practise. Choose one or two affirmations and repeat them to yourself over and over when you are feeling relaxed. When you practise your affirmation, start by saying it out loud and with confidence, even if you don't believe what you are saying. Practising will help you use this strategy automatically when you're feeling anxious or notice your negative thoughts.

Treating Stress and Anxiety © 2008 Crown House Publishing and Dr Lillian Nejad and Katerina Volny

Affirmations

The following are quotes, some serious and some amusing, that may serve as self-statements in times of stress.

Worry

- *If you can't sleep, then get up and do something instead of lying there and worrying. It's the worry that gets you, not the loss of sleep.* Dale Carnegie

- *Worry is interest paid on trouble before it falls due.* Dean W. R. Inge

- *Why is it, that no matter how busy we are, we always find time to worry?* P. K. Shaw

- *For every feared thing there is an opposing hope that encourages us.* Umberto Eco

- *The torment of precautions often exceeds the dangers to be avoided.* Napoleon I

- *One doesn't discover new lands without consenting to lose sight of the shore for a very long time.* André Gide

- *How irritating is someone with less intelligence but more nerve than we have.* W. G. Plunkett.

- *Half the things that people do not succeed in, are through fear of making the attempt.* James Northcote

Acceptance

- *What's done is done, it cannot be changed. Love not for the past, but for what lies ahead.* Darren Domin and Tim Page

- *Every path has its puddle.* English proverb

- *Life can only be understood backwards, but it must be lived forwards.* Søren Kierkegaard

- *Although the world is full of suffering, it is full also of the overcoming of it.* Helen Keller

- *The way I see it, if you want the rainbow, you gotta put up with the rain.* Dolly Parton

- *I can't change the direction of the wind, but I can adjust my sails to always reach my destination.* Jimmy Dean

- *Peace of mind is a mental condition in which you have accepted the worst.* Lin Yutang

- *You can clutch the past so tightly to your chest that it leaves your arms too full to embrace the present.* Jan Glidewell

- *If I try to be like him, who will be like me?* Yiddish proverb

- *Pure and complete sorrow is as impossible as pure and complete joy.* Leo Trotsky

Motivation

- *Action is the antidote to despair.* Joan Baez

- *We all find time to do what we really want to do.* William Feather

- *Do or do not, there is no try.* Yoda

- *No one knows what he can't do until he tries.* Anonymous

- *Chance favours the prepared mind.* Louis Pasteur

- *I always wondered why somebody doesn't do something about that. Then I realised I was somebody.* Lily Tomlin

- *Thoughts are useless unless followed by action.* P. K. Shaw

- *There are two mistakes one can make along the road to truth—not going all the way and not starting.* Buddha

- *Putting off an easy thing makes it hard. Putting off a hard thing makes it impossible.* W. G. Plunkett.

- *Don't wait for the light to appear at the end of the tunnel; stride down there … and light the bloody thing yourself!* Sara Henderson

- *The reward for a thing well done is to have done it.* Ralph Waldo Emerson

- *He has half the deed done who has made a beginning.* Horace

- *If we did all the things we are capable of doing, we would literally astound ourselves.* Thomas Edison

- *A journey of a thousand miles must begin with a single step.* Chinese proverb

- *The best advice we ever had was given us as toddlers: take one step at a time.* P. K. Shaw

- *Nothing can be created from nothing.* Lecretius

- *A final incentive before giving up a difficult task, try to imagine it successfully accomplished by someone you violently dislike.* K. Zenios

Support

- *Trouble is part of life, and if you don't share it, you don't give the person who loves you a chance to love you enough.* Dinah Shore

- *A friend is one who knows all about you but likes you just the same.* W. G. Plunkett.

- *Many a family tree needs trimming.* Kin Hubbard

- *Advice is what we ask for when we already know the answer but wish we didn't.* Erica Jong

- *Kind words can be short and easy to speak, but their echoes are truly endless.* Mother Theresa

- *One kind word can warm three winter months.* Japanese proverb

- *Words can sometimes, in moments of grace, attain the quality of deeds.* Elie Weisel

Treating Stress and Anxiety © 2008 Crown House Publishing and Dr Lillian Nejad and Katerina Volny

Problem solving

- *The best way to solve problems is not to create them.* P. K. Shaw

- *Do what you can, with what you have, where you are.* Theodore Roosevelt

- *A mixture of empathy and brainstorming can move mountains.* Hazel Hawke

- *The shortest way to do many things is to do only one thing at once.* Samuel Smiles

Change

- *Progress is impossible without change; and those who cannot change their minds cannot change anything.* George Bernard Shaw

- *Change is not made without inconvenience, even from worse to better.* Richard Hooker

- *Time may heal all wounds, but steady daily routine makes good bandages.* W. G. Plunkett.

- *All things good to know are difficult to learn.* Green proverb

- *He who does anything because it is custom, makes no choice.* John Stuart Mill

Overcoming obstacles and learning from mistakes

- *Failure is the condiment that gives success its flavour.* Truman Capote

- *Perfection has one grave defect; it is apt to be dull.* W. Somerset Maugham

- *Even a mistake may turn out to be the one thing necessary to a worthwhile achievement.* Henry Ford

- *There is only one thing more painful than learning from experience and that is not learning from experience.* Archibald McLeish

- *Learn from the mistakes of others—you can never live long enough to make them all yourself.* Martin Luther King

- *Insight, plus hindsight, equals foresight.* Russell Murphy

- *When written in Chinese, the word crisis is composed of two characters. One represents danger and the other represents opportunity.* John F. Kennedy

- *Although the world is full of suffering, it is also full of the overcoming of it.* Helen Keller

- *We will either find a way, or make one!* Hannibal

- *He who never made a mistake never made a discovery.* Samuel Smiles

Handout 6.5   Page 3 of 3

Chapter 7

Facing fears

Avoidance of anxiety-provoking situations and the relief that it brings reinforces and strengthens anxiety symptoms. Breaking the anxiety, avoidance, and relief cycle is essential to treat anxiety and is achieved through exposure to anxiety-provoking situations for a sufficient amount of time to allow the anxiety symptoms to decrease. Each time exposure occurs in this way the anxiety symptoms decrease because it provides an opportunity for the individual to learn that the situation does not lead to terrible outcomes. Education about anxiety is essential to this process as it provides clients with the rationale and motivation to face feared or distressing situations (see Handout 7.1).

The process of facing fears to overcome anxiety and panic is termed "exposure therapy". This process involves repeated exposure to a feared situation until the level of anxiety experienced is reduced to a level of low to no distress. Exposure to anxiety-provoking situations is often planned in a graded manner, so that the client begins with a situation that provokes a small amount of anxiety and gradually increases to more anxiety-provoking situations. An important aim of exposure therapy is for the individual to learn that the feared situation is not harmful (even though it feels like it is); therefore, it is necessary to allow enough time for the distress experienced during an exposure task to subside to a low level.

Although some approaches contend that immediate exposure to the feared situation is more effective and efficient (e.g., Wilson, 2003), graduated or graded exposure to feared situations is the most common method of exposure therapy. Graded exposure is also generally favoured by clients for the obvious reason that it is especially distressing and difficult to face a very intense fear.

The first step in graded exposure is the collaborative development of a hierarchy of feared situations from low-intensity fear to high-intensity fear. The client then rates each situation using the SUDS or subjective units of distress scale from 0 (no anxiety or distress) to 100 (extreme anxiety or distress). For example, if a person has a specific phobia of spiders they may start by looking at a picture of a spider (SUDS 30), then being in the presence of a spider (SUDS 70), and then go on to move a spider from one place to another (SUDS 100). Worksheet 7.1 can be utilised to help clients develop their hierarchy. Clients will need assistance in making each level in the hierarchy as specific as possible and ensuring that there are enough steps towards their goal. The top of the hierarchy does not need to be the scariest situation they can think of regarding the feared situation (e.g., letting a spider crawl on my face) but should reflect the client's goal regarding the situation (e.g., be able to pick up a spider with a tissue and take it outside).

Once the hierarchy is established, the individual then faces these situations one at a time until the distress decreases. This task is repeated until the distress rating is consistently low when facing this fear. SUDS ratings can be recorded at regular intervals (every three minutes) during the exposure to assess the change in distress over time. The client can either go through the hierarchy on their own and use sessions to discuss successes and barriers to success with their therapist or the therapist can directly assist them in exposure by accompanying the client and providing direction and motivation as needed. Worksheet 7.2 can assist clients to monitor strategies that they use to reduce anxiety before, during, and after exposure tasks.

Other anxiety management techniques like relaxation exercises (Chapter 5) and coping statements (Chapter 6) can assist an individual to tolerate exposure to anxiety. The process of substituting a relaxation response for a feared response in graded exposure is called systematic desensitisation. However, some approaches caution managing anxiety through behavioural or cognitive means because they may interfere with habituation (Wells, 1997; Wilson, 2003). For example, if the aim of the exposure task is to reduce fears associated with harm related to their anxiety symptoms ("I will lose control," "I will have a heart attack"), then controlling the anxiety during exposure can interfere with this goal. In other words, not pairing exposure with anxiety management practices leads to the discovery that anxiety will diminish with exposure to a situation for a long enough duration. However, it may be unrealistic to expect clients not to use any strategies to manage their anxiety during exposure tasks whether you direct them to or not. Consider your own therapeutic style, the patient's attitudes, and the aims of the exposure task when deciding whether to pair exposure with anxiety management practices.

If a client is so fearful that they are unlikely or unwilling to attempt graded exposure in real situations, then imaginal exposure may be a useful preliminary step. Imaginal exposure usually involves systematic desensitisation and teaching the client relaxation techniques. Once the client can achieve a deep state of relaxation, the therapist asks the client to imagine a peaceful and safe scene in as much detail as possible. Then, the therapist describes the feared situation in detail while the client imagines it in order to elicit the anxiety response. The client is instructed to give SUDS ratings during this process and if mild to moderate anxiety is indicated, the client uses relaxation techniques to reduce anxiety and may return to the peaceful scene. When the client is fully relaxed, the feared situation is reintroduced. If the client experiences strong anxiety, the relaxation response is elicited immediately by returning to the peaceful scene.

The client continues to go back and forth until the distress subsides in the feared situation. Worksheet 7.1 describes this process in detail for the client.

Facing fears is a challenging endeavour that requires a great deal of effort. When individuals attempt to reduce their long-term anxiety by facing their fears, some degree of discomfort and distress in the short term is to be expected. When considering the viability of exposure therapy it is helpful to consider several factors, including the level of dysfunction that the fear causes, the individual's perception of the level of dysfunction that the fear causes, and the motivation of the individual to overcome the fear. For people with complex difficulties or those who have lived with fears for a long time, spend considerable time educating them about the nature of anxiety, how fears are maintained and how fears can generalise to more situations, and then help them consider the pros and cons of treating the anxiety. It can also be helpful to assist them in understanding the origin of their anxiety so that they can understand how the situation developed.

Fear and anxiety serve a useful function in signalling and responding to threats, and avoidance can sometimes be an adaptive response essential for safety and survival. Therefore, before undertaking steps to eliminate fear through exposure techniques, it is appropriate to consider if the individual's fear has a helpful role to play. For example, a person may be fearful of driving a car after an accident and, if the accident was related to the individual's alcohol use or sleep deprivation, the anxiety they feel may be useful in promoting safer driving practices in the future.

As exposure therapy is a difficult task and can seem counterintuitive to an anxious person, education about the nature of anxiety and the rationale for anxiety treatment is essential. Refer to Chapter 1 handouts for general education about anxiety. Handouts and worksheets in this chapter describe the rationale and process of exposure therapy.

Why is it important to face your fears?
The role of avoidance

Facing fear is difficult and at times may not seem like such a good idea. However, facing fears reduces and can even eliminate fears, while continuing to avoid fears makes them stronger. The following outlines an example of the process in which avoidance strengthens fears.

Step 1	Person experiences a perceived fear	"If I go out driving I might have an accident. I could get hurt or die."
Step 2	Arousal and anxiety at the thought of facing the fear	Increase in heart rate, breathing, muscle tension, perspiration, stomach ache, frightening thoughts.
Step 3	Avoidance	A decision is made not to go out driving on this occasion.
Step 4	Relief at avoiding the perceived threat	The symptoms of anxiety and arousal subside.
Step 5	Reinforcement and strengthening of the perceived fear	At the next opportunity to go out driving, the individual has learned that avoidance results in relief of distressing symptoms, and therefore, avoidance seems like a good idea.
Step 6	Person experiences a fear in another situation and the avoidance response is generalised.	Person uses avoidance to deal with fear because of previous experience that this strategy reduces distress at least in the short-term.

Avoidance of one fear can lead to other fears emerging

In some cases, when distressing anxiety and panic symptoms develop, fear of one situation can lead to fear of other situations. For example, a person that became fearful of driving after experiencing an accident may later become fearful of travelling in any mode of transport (bus, train, airplane, walking) and then become fearful of going anywhere. Even if the fear is extremely unlikely or unrealistic, the experience of symptoms of anxiety make it seem real. Just the possibility of experiencing anxiety and panic symptoms can sometimes convince people to avoid a situation. In these circumstances, the focus is no longer on worrying that you may be in an accident (as in the above example), but that you may experience anxiety about being in an accident—it is fearing fear itself.

Facing the fear, while managing the anxiety symptoms, breaks the cycle of anxiety by demonstrating that the situation is not going to lead to disaster.

How to face your fear effectively

- Learn about and understand your anxiety
- Develop some skills to manage anxiety and panic symptoms
  - use relaxation and breathing exercises
  - manage your thoughts with more helpful thoughts
- Decide to face your fear
- Plan to face your fear by developing a fear hierarchy
- Face your fear until your distress decreases
- Monitor and evaluate your progress

The graph below illustrates how distress decreases each time an individual completes an exposure to their fear.

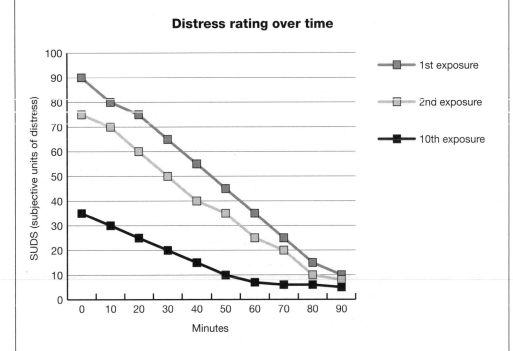

As you face your fear repeatedly you will notice that the level of distress you experience decreases in intensity and duration. It is essential to remain in the feared situation until your level of distress decreases so that you learn that the situation and your anxiety symptoms are not harmful.

Handout 7.1   Page 2 of 2

Preparing to face your fear

Deciding to face your fear

Deciding to face your fear is an important step. Consider the benefits and difficulties that are involved in facing your fear. How would your life be different if you could do the things that you now avoid without overwhelming fear and distress? What kind of commitment of time and effort will this take? Do you have adequate supports and resources to tackle this task?

Benefits	Difficulties

This list will help you to make an effective decision. If you decide to face your fear you can use this list to remind you of the reasons for doing it.

Describing the intensity of your fear

In order to plan to face fears in a graded manner, it is important to be able to rate the level of fear that situations may provoke. You can think of your distress as something that can be measured by a thermometer—100 units of distress is the most extreme distress imaginable and 0 units of distress is no discomfort. Measuring distress on a scale in relation to feared situations is called SUDS (subjective units of distress scale).

SUDS

100	extreme distress
90	
80	very high distress
70	
60	high distress
50	
40	moderate distress
30	
20	mild distress
10	
0	no distress

Treating Stress and Anxiety © 2008 Crown House Publishing and Dr Lillian Nejad and Katerina Volny

Developing a hierarchy of fears

Identify between four to fifteen tasks that trigger varying levels of fear and distress. These tasks can include imagining doing an anxiety-provoking task as well as actually doing it. See the information below about imaginal exposure.

Rank the tasks from the highest to lowest level of distress. Start with a scene that creates the mildest instance of anxiety. Then think of a scene that creates the strongest anxiety reaction and which is the most challenging—this is usually your goal. Now, fill in the steps in-between and rate your level of distress related to each step according to the SUDS. Consider the anxiety that you experience in anticipation of each task as well.

The process of exposure begins with facing a situation, through visualisation or in reality, that currently causes you moderate anxiety. You are to stay in the situation until your distress decreases and continue to repeat the task until your anxiety is consistently low when facing this fear. You can then move on to the next step in your hierarchy.

Fear hierarchy

Level of distress	SUDS	Feared situation
Extreme distress		
Very high distress		
High distress		
Moderate distress		
Mild distress		

Using imaginal exposure

Sometimes the anxiety associated with facing your fears is so high it can deter you from doing anything about it. If this is the case with you, consider starting to expose yourself to feared situations in your imagination. This is called imaginal exposure. A therapist can help you learn the techniques that will help you relax and cope during this process.

Success depends on four things:

1. Capacity to attain a deep state of relaxation
2. Creation of an appropriate hierarchy from mildly to very anxiety-provoking situations
3. Ability to vividly visualise your anxiety-provoking and peaceful scenes
4. Practice and patience

The process of imagery desensitisation

Step 1: Practise relaxation techniques and learn to attain a deep state of relaxation.

Step 2: Imagine your peaceful and safe scene—be as detailed as possible: objects, colours, light, sounds, temperature, smells, tastes, emotions, etc.

Step 3: Desensitisation involves first relaxing, then imagining your peaceful scene, then visualising the situation in your hierarchy one by one until you feel little or no anxiety.

- If you start to experience mild to moderate anxiety, try breathing techniques, calming affirmations ("I am calm and at ease with myself") and picture yourself handling the situation calmly, then go back to the peaceful scene until you are fully relaxed.

- Once you are fully relaxed again, go back to the situation. Keep doing this until you are relaxed in that situation.

- If you experience extremely strong anxiety take yourself immediately to the peaceful scene.

- You need to be fully comfortable with each step before you advance.

- If the step continues to cause too much anxiety, put an intermediate step in-between.

Monitoring your fear

1. Describe the task:

_____

_____

_____

2. Describe your skills to manage symptoms of anxiety (before, during, and after the task)

   Relaxation and breathing exercises:

   _____

   _____

   _____

   Strategies to manage distressing thoughts:

   _____

   _____

   _____

Chart your distress over time:

Time	SUDS (0 to 100)
Just before (0 mins)	
1 minute	
2 minutes	
5 minutes	
10 minutes	
20 minutes	
30 minutes	
40 minutes	
50 minutes	
60 minutes	
90 minutes	

Review changes in distress over time:

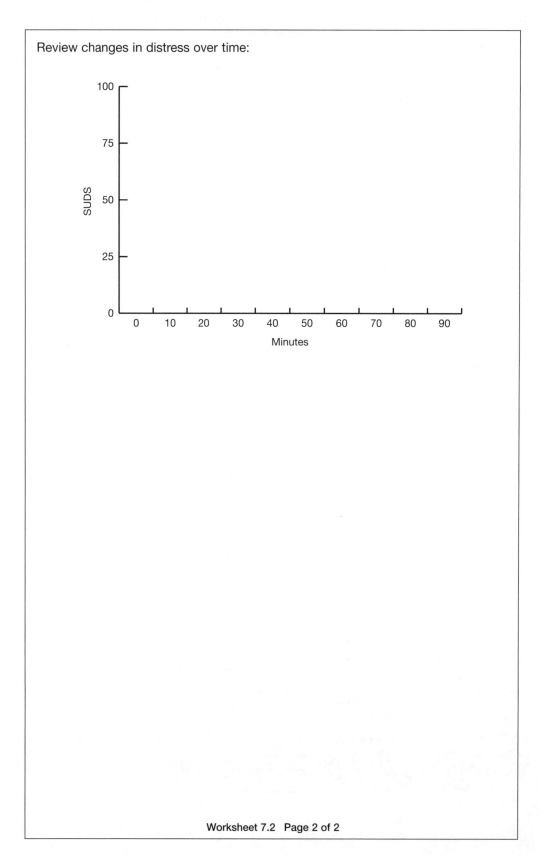

Worksheet 7.2   Page 2 of 2

Chapter 8

Relapse prevention

Recovering from any illness, physical or emotional, or changing long-standing patterns of thoughts and behaviours takes time and people experience ups and downs along the way. Clients are likely to have setbacks during their treatment (e.g., reverting to avoidance strategies, having panic attacks) and it is important for them to know that this is a normal part of the change process. It is also vital for them to be aware that setbacks are likely to occur throughout their lives and the way they think about these setbacks will influence how they respond to them. For instance, if a client has a panic attack and he starts reverting to old thought patterns like, "I'll never get better," "I am so weak," "I can't cope with this," the likelihood of a downward spiral and a full relapse increases. However, if he were to think, "This was just a panic attack," "I know how to manage my anxiety," "Setbacks are normal," then he is more likely to recover quickly from the episode.

Discussing the likelihood of setbacks, spending some time predicting their occurrence, and planning the most helpful responses are important components of the final stages of the treatment process. Clients need to know that there are ways to reduce the impact of setbacks and to prevent full relapses, including:

- Identifying and monitoring early warning signs
- Being aware of situations that cause stress and anxiety
- Being aware of what increases vulnerability to stress and anxiety
- Acknowledging strengths that can assist in managing stress and anxiety
- Regularly practising new skills
- Taking medication as prescribed
- Maintaining and/or building support networks
- Accessing resources in the community
- Developing a relapse prevention plan (see Worksheet 8.1 for a relapse prevention plan template)

See Handout 8.2 for ways to reduce the impact and frequency of relapses for clients.

Identifying and monitoring early warning signs

If your client has a moderate to severe anxiety disorder, identifying the early warning signs of the disorder is recommended. Early warning signs are changes in feelings, thinking, or behaviour that signal that the anxiety is starting to take hold again. These changes often happen slowly and can be noticed well ahead of an actual relapse.

Common early signs are: changes in sleeping or eating patterns, isolation from others, difficulty concentrating, feeling more anxious or irritated than usual, avoidance behaviours, and being more unmotivated or less energetic than usual. Handout 8.1 lists triggers, early warning signs, and actions or coping strategies for clients.

When listing early warning signs, ensure that they are as specific as possible. For instance, if an early warning sign is less sleep, identify how many hours is "less" and how long this needs to continue for it to be considered an early warning sign. See Table 4 for some examples.

Table 4: Specifying early warning signs

General early warning sign	Specific early warning sign
Less sleep	Sleep 3–5 hours/night (rather than 6–9 hours/night) for more than five days
Don't go out	Don't go out with friends at the weekend for more than a month (usually go out once a week)
Feel more anxious	Anxiety levels go up to 8/10 or higher for more than three days (usual level 3–5/10)

It is often difficult for clients to remember the early feelings, thoughts, and behaviours that preceded their anxiety problem, so you might encourage them to ask family members or friends what they noticed.

The process of identifying early warning signs should be empowering rather than frightening. Your clients will be leaving therapy with new skills, new thought patterns, and a sense of confidence in their ability to cope; therefore, if early warning signs appear they will be more equipped to manage their symptoms. Decide together what symptoms are expected and easily managed, versus what symptoms over what period of time would signal a potential relapse, and the steps the client will take if that occurs.

Being aware of situations that cause stress and anxiety

Clients, as well as their therapists, can often predict when they are likely to have a setback, particularly with recurrent stressors in their lives. Together you can plan a strategy for these situations. Common situations that cause stress are relationship problems, loss of employment, meeting new people, and being around critical people.

Being aware of what increases vulnerability to stress and anxiety

Factors that increase people's vulnerability to stress and anxiety include being physically unwell, lacking sleep, being overworked, not maintaining a healthy lifestyle (diet, exercise), and not asserting their wants and needs. Ensure that your clients are aware that if they are feeling a heightened sense of tension, stress, or anxiety, they may need to take better care of themselves. They may not be able to change certain situations or people but they do have control over how they treat themselves and, therefore, can reduce their vulnerability to stress and anxiety.

Acknowledging strengths that can assist in managing stress and anxiety

Every client has a personal set of strengths that have helped them to cope, to interact with others, to ask for help, and to survive. Writing down the client's strengths as well as how they can help them through challenging times is a useful exercise.

Regularly practising new skills

In therapy, clients have learned new skills to help them manage stress and anxiety, both generally and in specific situations. It is often useful for the client to have a list they can refer to in order to remind them of the strategies that they find most effective in lowering their general level of tension and anxiety as well as managing stress, fear, and anxiety in specific situations. Since stress, anxiety, and fear are part of life, encourage your clients to continue to practise their skills on a regular basis to enhance their well-being and resilience as well as deal with the setbacks that will inevitably occur.

Taking medication as prescribed

If clients are taking prescribed medication, impress upon them the need to take the medication as prescribed and only reduce or increase it with a doctor's supervision. If they experience unpleasant side effects encourage them to speak to their prescribing doctor about it. Changes in medication of any kind can often be a trigger for increased stress.

Maintaining and/or building a support network

Support networks include all types of relationships—what is important is to develop and maintain relationships with people who are friendly, understanding, and supportive. It is helpful for clients to have a list of people to contact for support if they start noticing early warning signs or are finding it difficult to cope. Support networks may include family members, friends, GP, people in their local community, and co-workers.

Accessing resources in the community

Sometimes going straight from therapy to being on their own can be quite challenging for people. There are many resources in the community that can provide a supportive transition period or even ongoing support for your clients. Resources in the community include support groups, educational courses, social groups, telephone support, and counselling services. Encourage your clients to seek this information even if they don't want or need it now. You may also assist them by doing a search of the resources in your area and having a list that you can give to your clients.

Developing a prevention plan

While identifying early warning signs, stress triggers, vulnerabilities, coping strategies, and supports, it is useful for the client to write everything down in a clear and organised way with a view to putting it in a safe and easily accessible place. See Worksheet 8.1 for a prevention plan format.

List of possible triggers, early warning signs, and strategies

To prevent a relapse of any illness, it is useful to know what the possible triggers may be, what the early warning signs are for relapse, and what to do if early warning signs are present. Below is a list of triggers, early warning signs, and strategies to deal with relapse reported by other people who have experienced anxiety. You can use this as a guide to completing your own relapse prevention plan.

Possible triggers	Early warning signs	Strategies/action plan
• Overworked	• Severe negative thoughts	• Relaxation
• More pressures	• Worrying constantly	• Get help
• Meeting new people	• Ruminating thoughts	• Talk to family
• Being in a crowded public place	• Drinking	• Talk to a professional (GP, nurse, counsellor)
• Social situations	• Not talking to people	• Humour
• Public speaking	• Sleeping patterns change	• Positive affirmations
• Relationship problems	• Can't sit still	• Religious faith
• Financial difficulties	• Stop eating	• Hope
• Being in group or class-room settings	• Overeat	• Look at prevention plan
• Sharing personal thoughts	• Feel sad, depressed	• Sit quietly
• Family	• Feel scared, fearful	• Recreation
• Criticism from others	• Stay in room	• Take a walk
• Physical illness	• Don't go out	• Listen to music
	• People tell me: *"You're not well" "Calm down" "You need help"*	• Play with the dog
		• Watch TV
		• Do something you enjoy
		• Go to a movie
		• Face fear

Treating Stress and Anxiety © 2008 Crown House Publishing and Dr Lillian Nejad and Katerina Volny

Preventing relapse

Recovering from any illness, physical or emotional, or changing long-standing patterns of thoughts and behaviours takes time and people experience ups and downs along the way. Having setbacks both during and after therapy is a normal part of the change process. There are ways to reduce the impact of setbacks and prevent relapses from occurring including:

- Identifying and monitoring early warning signs
- Being aware of situations that cause stress and anxiety
- Being aware of what increases vulnerability to stress and anxiety
- Acknowledging strengths that can assist in managing stress and anxiety
- Regularly practising new skills
- Taking medication as prescribed
- Maintaining and/or building support networks
- Accessing resources in the community
- Developing a relapse prevention plan

Identifying and monitoring your early warning signs

Early warning signs are changes in feelings, thinking, or behaviour which signal that anxiety is starting to take hold again. These changes often happen slowly and can be noticed well ahead of an actual relapse.

Common early signs are: changes in sleeping or eating patterns, isolating yourself from others, difficulty concentrating, feeling more anxious or irritated than usual, avoidance behaviours, and being more unmotivated or less energetic than usual. Try to make your early warning signs as specific as possible—your therapist can help you with this.

It may be difficult for you to remember the early feelings, thoughts, and behaviours that preceded your anxiety problem. It may be helpful to ask your family members or friends the changes they noticed.

Your therapist will also be able to help you distinguish between symptoms that you can manage on your own and symptoms that signal the need for more help. In order to notice these signs it can be helpful to monitor them on a regular basis. Again, your family or friends can help you with this.

Being aware of situations that cause you stress

Stress is a part of life. However, if stress becomes too overwhelming or too intense it makes it difficult to manage your feelings, thoughts, behaviours, and life in general. Therefore, it is important to be aware of what situations cause you the most stress so that you can do something about it. Some situations that can cause stress are relationship problems, loss of employment, lacking a stable place to live, meeting new people, and being around critical people.

Stressful situations can trigger setbacks so it can be helpful to plan a strategy for these situations, especially if they are recurrent stressors in your life. See Handout 7.1 for examples of triggers, symptoms, and strategies.

Being aware of what increases vulnerability to stress and anxiety

Factors that can increase your vulnerability to stress and anxiety include being physically unwell, lacking sleep, being overworked, not maintaining a healthy lifestyle (diet, exercise), and not communicating your wants and needs. If you are feeling a heightened sense of tension, stress, or anxiety, this is probably a sign that you need to take better care of yourself. You may not be able to change certain situations or people but you do have control over how you treat yourself.

Acknowledging strengths that can assist in managing stress and anxiety

Everyone has a personal set of strengths that help them cope, interact with others, ask for help, and survive. Write down your strengths as well as how they have helped you in the past and how they can help you through challenging times in the future.

Regularly practising new skills

You have learned new skills to help you manage stress and anxiety, both generally and in specific situations. You probably found some strategies more helpful than others. Write down the skills and strategies that most effectively help you to manage your stress and anxiety so that you can refer to it whenever you need it. Some strategies you may have found helpful are talking to someone about it, limiting involvement with certain stressful situations or certain people, telling yourself that you can get through it, rewarding yourself for being able to manage your stress, practising breathing and relaxation exercises, sticking to a daily routine or planning your days, distracting yourself from distressing thoughts and feelings, and doing something pleasant and fun every day. Since stress, anxiety, and fear are part of life, it is important to continue to practise your new skills on a regular basis to enhance your well-being, improve your resilience, and deal with the setbacks that normally occur.

Taking medication as prescribed

If you are taking prescribed medication, take it as prescribed and only reduce or increase medication with a doctor's supervision. Some people experience unpleasant side effects from taking or discontinuing medication and it is important to talk to your doctor about this.

Building a support network

Support networks include all types of relationships—what is important is to develop and maintain relationships with people that are friendly, understanding, and supportive. It is helpful to have a list of people to contact for support if you start noticing early warning signs or you are finding it difficult to cope. Your support network may include family members, friends, GP, people in your local community, and people you work with.

Accessing resources in your community

Sometimes going straight from therapy to being on your own can be quite challenging and scary. There are many resources in the community that can provide you with a supportive transition period or even ongoing support. Resources in the community include support groups, educational courses, social groups, telephone support, and counselling services. Even if you think you don't need extra support, having the information readily available just in case is recommended. Your therapist may be able to assist you with appropriate options.

Developing a prevention plan

Once you have identified your early warning signs, stress triggers, and coping strategies and supports, it is useful to write it down in a clear and organised way. That way you will be able to refer back to it whenever you wish, you can show your plan to others, and you can take charge of your mental health. You can always make changes to your plan if necessary. See Worksheet 8.1 for ways to help you develop your own prevention plan. When you've finished filling it in, put it in a safe place where you can have easy access to it.

Prevention plan

Name: **Date:**

My early warning signs include (be as specific as possible: for instance, instead of writing "sleep less", write, "sleep less than four hours instead of my usual eight for more than five days"):

1. _____

2. _____

3. _____

4. _____

5. _____

Situations that tend to cause stress in my life are (again be specific, for instance instead of writing, "my relationship", write, "when I argue with my spouse over the finances"):

1. _____

2. _____

3. _____

4. _____

5. _____

I am more vulnerable to stress and anxiety when:

1. _____

2. _____

3. _____

4. _____

5. _____

Strengths that help me through challenging situations are:

1. _____

2. _____

3. _____

4. _____

5. _____

Skills and strategies that work for me in managing stress are:

1. _____

2. _____

3. _____

4. _____

5. _____

My current prescribed medication and dosage is:

_____

Side effects of my medication I'm going to talk to my doctor about are:

_____

_____

Support people I can turn to are:

1. _____

2. _____

3. _____

4. _____

5. _____

Worksheet 8.1   Page 2 of 2

Resources I can access in my community are:

1. _____

2. _____

3. _____

People to contact if I notice early warning signs or I'm having difficulty coping are:

Person	Contact number(s)
GP	
Psychologist/Counsellor	

Chapter 9

Other issues related to stress and anxiety

Stress and anxiety problems are often triggered, maintained, and exacerbated by other concerns, skills deficits, and co-morbid disorders. Issues often affecting stress and anxiety levels are poor sense of self, communication skills deficits, anger problems, substance use, and depressive symptoms. Strengthening identity, improving communication skills, and managing anger, as well as addressing substance abuse and depression, can be an important adjunct to stress and anxiety management. If problems of depression, substance abuse, or anger management are assessed to be the primary presenting problem, and are substantial, then specialised resource and treatment guidelines should be consulted or referral to a clinician or service experienced in treating the problem is required. For example, if an individual is intoxicated for much of the time they are unlikely to benefit from treatment for stress and anxiety management. Therefore, reducing or abstaining from substance use would be the primary target for therapy and may require specialised treatment.

Depression

Anxiety and depression can often present concurrently; therefore, providing psychoeducation to the client about depression symptoms and strategies to reduce depressive symptoms is useful. Handouts 9.1 and 9.2 provide education about depression and Handout 9.3 describes strategies to manage depression. Engaging in regular exercise, maintaining healthy sleep and wake routines, participating in pleasant activities, and challenging unhelpful thoughts are also important aspects of treatment for depression. Chapter 4 provides resources to enhance exercise, sleep, and pleasant activities. Chapter 7 provides strategies to manage unhelpful thoughts. An activity schedule is provided (Worksheet 9.1) to assist in the implementation of some activities, with the inclusion of a mood rating. This worksheet assists clients to observe relationships between activities and mood and also provides a means of assessing the individual's mood over time. Where persistent very low mood is present, assessment and treatment by a clinician experienced with depressive disorder is warranted.

Substance use

The one-year prevalence of individuals with an anxiety disorder and a co-morbid substance use disorder is up to 15% (Grant et al., 2004). Use of substances is a common strategy for managing symptoms associated with stress and anxiety. For instance, many people drink alcohol to help them sleep. While this strategy may provide some relief in the short term, frequent or excessive substance use may cause more stress and other difficulties in the long term. (In the case of sleep, alcohol usually helps people fall asleep but leads to disturbed sleep during the night.) Use of substances can also play a significant role in maintaining anxiety when they are used as a tool for avoiding the experience of anxiety symptoms. Therefore, reducing or abstaining from substance use may be a necessary preliminary step before anxiety treatment. A medical assessment and management of detoxification and withdrawal may also be required.

While an individual may be keen to work on stress and anxiety management, they may be reluctant to consider reducing substance use that they have been relying on for some time. Motivational interviewing strategies can assist a client to consider the impact of substance use and its benefits and drawbacks. Placing an emphasis on the client's own personal choice and eliciting their own concerns about this behaviour are the aims of motivational interviewing. The therapist assists the client to evaluate their own substance use comprehensively by assisting them to reflect on the impact of their use on themselves and others, and any changes in patterns of use that have occurred. Over time, if substantial drawbacks of substance use are noticed and acknowledged, compared to relatively few benefits, an individual may wish to commit to the goal of reducing or eliminating their substance use. Simply assisting an individual to thoroughly evaluate their substance use and consider whether this may be an important issue to address can be a very valuable role for a therapist to perform.

It can be helpful to consider the client's readiness to change their substance use in terms of Prochaska and DiClemente's (1983) stages of change model, as described in Chapter 2. Handout 9.4 provides a checklist to review the impact of substance use on an individual, and Worksheet 9.2 provides tools to review the advantages and disadvantages of substance use. If a reduction or elimination of substance use is identified as a goal for therapy then Handout 9.5 provides information about strategies to minimise or discontinue substance use, and Worksheet 9.3 is a diary to assist the individual to get to know their own substance use pattern of behaviour. Furthermore, if the client is using substances as a way of managing anxiety, consider teaching them some behavioural skills like relaxation exercises to ensure that they have other ways of coping with anxiety symptoms during the process of reducing or ceasing substance use. Consider referral to specialised treatment if substance abuse is the primary issue that is impacting on their psychological distress, quality of life, and functioning.

Self-acceptance and strengthening identity

A poor sense of self can both be a precursor and outcome of ongoing levels of high stress and difficulties. Individuals who do not have a strong or stable identity are both more vulnerable to and less resilient to setbacks in functioning due to trauma, grief, depression, anxiety, or mental illness. Ongoing or prolonged stress and anxiety can lead to decreased self-confidence and increased fear, even after the period of crisis or illness has passed, and personal strengths are often minimised or not acknowledged.

An important aspect of recovery is to reclaim positive aspects of the individual's life, character, and aspirations. It is important not only to survive a period of crisis or illness but also to enjoy fully participating in life again. It is also helpful to reframe difficult experiences as opportunities for the individual to learn about personal strengths and weaknesses and to re-evaluate goals. Handout 9.6 provides some guidelines to rebuilding identity, increasing confidence, and establishing goals for the future.

Anger

Anger is another emotion that can be both beneficial and problematic. Clients who experience problematic anger may be reluctant to identify this as something they want to change. Reviewing their experience and the consequences of anger may be helpful. People experiencing anxiety and depression may also experience an increase in anger as their anxiety and depressive symptoms decrease. Handout 9.7 describes helpful and problematic aspects of anger, Handout 9.8 reviews common experiences of anger, and Handout 9.9 provides some strategies for changing the experience of anger.

Communication skills

Effective communication is essential to working towards goals and managing relationships. It is also important to have assertiveness skills to manage conflictual interpersonal interactions. Handout 9.10 describes various communication styles and provides some guidelines for planning assertive communication.

What is depression?

Depression is a term that is often used to describe feelings of sadness ("the blues") or grief which most of us experience from time to time. This form of depression is often a reaction to stressful events and usually lasts for a short time.

When does a normal case of "having the blues" become a problem?

When a person feels sad *and* experiences a range of physical (fatigue, change in appetite), behavioural (low motivation, withdrawal from social activities), emotional (feelings of sadness, hopelessness) and cognitive (negative or self-critical thoughts) symptoms, he or she may be experiencing a more severe form of depression. If these symptoms interfere with a person's normal routine and their relationships, if the pain and problems associated with the symptoms outweigh pleasure most of the time, and if the symptoms last for two weeks, it is important to seek help.

What are the causes of depression?

There is no single cause of depression. Usually several factors influence the development of depression:

- **Heredity**: Depression can run in families.
- **Biological influences**: Hormonal or chemical imbalances in the brain can influence mood and can result in depression. Illness, infection, alcohol, and other drugs can also lead to changes in the brain that affect mood.
- **Stress**: Personal tragedies or disasters, childbirth, loss of employment, menopause, retirement, and other stressful events can contribute to the onset of depression. People who experience prolonged stress over time due to repeated losses and stress throughout their life can lose hope and feel helpless and depressed.
- **Personality**: People who set unrealistic standards for themselves and others and find it difficult to adjust these expectations in various circumstances are at risk of becoming depressed. Also, people who have difficulty expressing themselves and their needs, and therefore do not get their needs met, may develop depression.

What can you do about it?

Even though depression can be overwhelming, there are several treatments that are highly successful. The type of treatment depends on the type of depression and how severe it is. According to research, a combination of psychological and medical treatment is the most effective intervention for depression.

Treating Stress and Anxiety © 2008 Crown House Publishing and Dr Lillian Nejad and Katerina Volny

Psychological treatment

There are a range of psychological treatments that are effective in treating depression. Cognitive behavioural therapy (CBT) is one such treatment that aims to increase helpful behaviours and change unhelpful thought patterns. Counselling can also assist people to help themselves in current and future situations by learning a range of techniques, such as relaxation, communication skills, problem-solving, and goal setting.

Anti-depressant medication

Medication can relieve depression, restore normal sleep patterns and appetite, and reduce anxiety by bringing the chemicals in the brain back into balance. You may experience some side effects but these medications are not addictive. Your doctor or psychiatrist will assess your individual situation to ascertain whether medication is a useful intervention. Remember that a combination of psychological and medical treatment is often the most effective intervention. Medication will treat your symptoms, but it will not help you find solutions to your difficulties or help you learn effective coping skills to manage and reduce current and future depressive symptoms.

Electro convulsive treatment (ECT)

This can be a highly effective treatment for more severe forms of depression that are not responding to psychological and other medical treatment.

Transcranial magnetic stimulation (TMS)

This is an emerging treatment with consistent positive outcomes in research studies but is not yet commonly used. It involves the use of strong magnetic fields to stimulate the brain. This occurs while the person is awake and alert and no anaesthetic is used.

The effects of depression

Listed below are some of the common effects of depression. As you can see, there are many effects associated with depression which can be divided into four categories: physical effects, effects to do with thinking, emotional effects, and behavioural effects. Place a '✓' next to the ones you can relate to.

Physical	Thinking	Feeling	Behaviour
❑ Fatigue	❑ I am worthless	❑ Sad	❑ Crying
❑ Lack of energy	❑ I deserve to be punished	❑ Depressed	❑ Slowing down
❑ Unexplained headaches, back-aches, etc.	❑ I want to die	❑ Irritable	❑ Neglecting responsibilities
❑ Digestive problems	❑ I can't cope	❑ Anxious	❑ Lack of self-care
❑ Loss or increase of appetite	❑ Everybody hates me	❑ Fearful	❑ Neglecting appearance
❑ Weight loss or weight gain	❑ Nothing is fun anymore	❑ Guilty	❑ Low motivation
❑ Loss of sex drive	❑ I am to blame for everything	❑ Hopeless	❑ Withdrawal from others
❑ Decrease or increase in sleep	❑ Only bad things will happen to me	❑ Helpless	❑ Decrease social activities
	❑ Nobody can help me	❑ Flat	❑ Suicide attempts
	❑ I will stay like this forever	❑ Numb	❑ Stopping eating/overeating
	❑ Difficulty concentrating	❑ Empty	❑ Sleeping problems
	❑ Poor memory	❑ Can't feel pleasure	❑ Not laughing about things that used to be funny
		❑ Apathy	❑ Decrease in libido

Strategies to manage depression

There are several techniques* that anybody can learn, with or without professional help, that will help manage and reduce depressive symptoms. Some strategies are introduced below.

Revisiting pleasurable activities

Depression often leads to feeling unmotivated and losing interest in pleasurable activities. However, withdrawing from others and not participating in interests and hobbies usually makes people feel guilty and more depressed—it's a vicious cycle. Therefore, it is important to do things you like even though you don't feel like it. Remember that motivation builds after you do something, not before—so don't wait to feel motivated. Instead, force yourself to do something you used to enjoy and then notice your positive feelings afterwards that come from achieving something, no matter how small. It is often difficult to think of what to do when you are feeling down so below are some suggestions:

On your own	At home	To be active
Write	Garden	Walk
Play a game	Handy work	Run
Sing to music	Move furniture	Rollerblade
Draw or paint	Sew	Bike
Knit	Clean	Any sport
Woodwork	Make a cake	Stretch gently
Read	Play with pets	Swim
Jigsaw puzzle	Listen to music	Play ping-pong
View favourite photos	Take a bath	Golf
	Watch TV	Fish
Away from home	**Socially**	**To treat yourself**
Beach	Phone a friend	Massage
Cinema	Visit a friend	Facial
Zoo	Dinner guests	Bath
Shop	Restaurant	Hairdresser
Library	Gym	Do fingernails
Museum	Go out to lunch	Eat favourite food
Go to football	Join a class	Buy flowers
Bookshop	Play with kids	Take a break
Theatre	Have friends over to watch	Have a picnic
Cafe	video/DVD	

Challenging negative self-talk

Often when people are depressed they think negative thoughts that are sometimes unrealistic or overly critical. It is important to identify these thought patterns and challenge them by asking yourself whether they are true or just a symptom of depression. This can be difficult to do on your own and if this is the case, a psychologist or a counsellor can help. Examples of some common unhelpful thought patterns are (see Handout 6.2 for descriptions of other unhelpful thought patterns):

- All-or-nothing thinking: "It must be perfect, or I'm a complete failure."
- Jumping to conclusions: "They must be laughing at me."
- Disqualifying the positive: "You're only saying that to be polite."
- Catastrophising: "If I don't get this job, it will be the end of the world."
- Should statements: "I should be able to cope."

Affirmations

These are positive statements that you say to yourself to replace negative thoughts or worries. Examples of affirmations are (see Handout 6.5 for more affirmations):

- "I accept the natural ups and downs of life."
- "It's never too late to change. I am improving one step at a time."
- "I love and accept myself the way I am."

In order for affirmations to help, you have to practise. Choose one or two affirmations and repeat them to yourself over and over when you are feeling relaxed. When you practise your affirmation, start by saying it out loud and with confidence, even if you don't believe what you are saying. Practising will help you use this strategy automatically when you're depressed or notice your negative thoughts.

Exercise

Exercise on its own has been shown to be effective in improving mood. The amount of exercise that is required is a half hour of exercise three times per week that increases your heart rate. Consider a brisk walk, swimming, or playing a team sport. See Handout 4.3 on using exercise to enhance your mood.

---

*For more information about these or other techniques refer to self-help books on depression that are widely available or consult a psychologist or counsellor experienced in this area.

Handout 9.3   Page 2 of 2

Improve your mood:
scheduling activities and monitoring mood

Schedule activities twice per day, and rate your mood before and after each activity. Choose activities that you find pleasant and that you are reasonably good at. Choose one physically active activity per day.

Rate your mood from 0 (feeling extremely down and negative) to 10 (feeling very happy and positive).

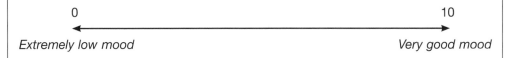

	Activity AM	Mood rating		Activity PM	Mood rating	
		Before	After		Before	After
Mon						
Tues						
Wed						
Thurs						
Fri						
Sat						
Sun						

Treating Stress and Anxiety © 2008 Crown House Publishing and Dr Lillian Nejad and Katerina Volny

Substance use and abuse: when is it too much?

Use of substances, drugs, or alcohol is a common and often socially accepted or encouraged behaviour. But when is it too much? You may have found what was once fun and under control has now become a way to help you escape from life's problems. You may not know any other ways of dealing with stress, and alcohol and other drugs provide short but immediate relief. You may not think or want to face that your substance use has become problematic but others have expressed concern about it. If you are unsure if your substance use is a problem for you, check out some of the warning signs of excessive substance below:

- You use substances to regularly relax, relieve anxiety, or go to sleep
- You use substances to cope with difficult tasks or social situations
- You socialise mostly with other regular substance users
- The amount of drugs or alcohol that you need to get the same effect has increased
- You can't stop using substances for more than a few days
- You feel guilty about your substance use
- You use substances in the morning to get going
- You can't remember periods of time while using substances
- You can't get things done because of substance use
- People who care about you are concerned about your substance use
- You use money meant for other expenses to pay for substances
- You take risks with substance use (driving, using machinery, looking after children, using while pregnant)
- You keep your substance use a secret (from significant others, GP)
- You are less responsible

General guidelines for amount of alcohol use:

- Women: More than seven drinks per week and more than three drinks per occasion is too much.
- Men: More than fourteen drinks per week and more than four drinks per occasion is too much.

Reviewing your substance use

Pros and cons

What are the benefits of substance use? e.g. mood change, forget worries, more confidence, social contact	What are the disadvantages of substance use? e.g. hangover, not available for some people, tasks, financial costs, health concerns

Some pros and cons may have more weight than others, so you may give them more emphasis. Consider all the pros and all the cons; if your cons outweigh the pros, then you are probably ready to do something about cutting down or eliminating your substance use. Pros and cons can change over time, so this list can be reviewed regularly.

Substance use goals

What are your goals for your substance use?

_____

_____

_____

_____

_____

- Do you need information about your substance use?
- Do you need to ask friends, family, or co-workers about their ideas about your substance use?
- Would it be helpful to keep a diary of your use to evaluate how much you are using?

Treating Stress and Anxiety © 2008 Crown House Publishing and Dr Lillian Nejad and Katerina Volny

Strategies to cut down or stop substance use

Get to know your substance use

People often underestimate their substance use. To get a more accurate picture, write down when you use, how much you use, and in what situations. You can also learn more about why you use by noting the thoughts, emotions, and behaviours that occur with substance use. The more you know about your substance use, the easier it will be to change this pattern of behaviour.

Eliminate triggers

- Avoid situations that are closely associated with substance use, especially when first trying to cut down or reduce substance use. If you use socially, plan alternative social events with people who don't use or in situations where using does not occur. For example, go to the movies instead of a drinking venue. If quiet times are when you use, plan to be around someone or even talk on the phone or plan something to keep you busy with a task.

- Plan and practise what to say and do if someone invites you to use substances.

- Remember that cravings pass with time. Plan things to do that are pleasant or that occupy you mentally or physically to distract yourself from cravings. Do some physical exercise, talk to someone, watch a movie, have a bath or shower, read a book.

- One day at a time, and one minute at a time. Set yourself a goal to delay using for a short period of time. When you succeed in getting through this period of time, set a goal for another period of time.

Change unhelpful thoughts

Identify unhelpful and unrealistic thoughts that may lead you to a decision to use substances. Such negative thoughts may be, "I'll never be able to change" or "What's the point?" Remind yourself that you have made a decision to reduce or stop using substances, and that this is because you deserve and can achieve positive goals in your life. It may be helpful to write down and frequently look at your reasons for changing your substance use and your goals for the future.

Manage emotions

Plan and practise using alternative strategies to manage stress and difficult emotions. Remind yourself that emotions are temporary, they come and go. Learn relaxation exercises, have a list of pleasant activities to provide a distraction, ask supportive friends or family members to be available to spend time with you or talk to you at times of difficulty. Seek professional assistance to solve difficult problems that cause ongoing stress, such as financial, legal, or relationship difficulties.

Treating Stress and Anxiety © 2008 Crown House Publishing and Dr Lillian Nejad and Katerina Volny

Reduce availability of substances and money

• Don't go to places where you can obtain the substances.

• Plan to spend or allocate your money every payday so that you cannot access money easily to buy substances. You could enlist the help of a friend or family member to manage your money or put your money into a bank account that requires you to go to the bank to withdraw it.

Plan alternative, less harmful behaviours

Substance use occurs because, to some extent, this behaviour has benefits. For example, it may relieve stress, worries, and boredom or provide social connections. When considering reducing or discontinuing substance use, it is important to plan alternatives to replace the function of substance use for you. Learning new skills like relaxation exercises or problem solving and participating in other pleasurable activities or interests is often helpful.

Two steps forward, one step back ...

• Some relapse of substance use is expected. If you use more than you planned it can be helpful to notice this and review your substance use goals as soon as possible. Rather than dwelling on relapse as a failure, use it as an opportunity to learn more about your pattern of use. Review the factors that encouraged you to use and plan alternative coping strategies for the next time a similar situation occurs.

• Remember to reward yourself for every reduction in your substance use. Every step forward is a success and brings realistic hope for further change.

Worksheet 9.3

Getting to know your substance use patterns

Getting to know your patterns of substance use is an important step in improving your management of them. Keep a record of times that you use substances or that you feel tempted to use substances.

Situation (triggers and vulnerabilities)	Thoughts and images	Physical feelings	Emotional feelings	Craving (0 to 10)	Behaviour

134

Treating Stress and Anxiety © 2008 Crown House Publishing and Dr Lillian Nejad and Katerina Volny

Self-acceptance and strengthening identity

Ongoing levels of high stress, breakdown, or setbacks in functioning due to trauma, grief, depression, anxiety, or mental illness can cause decreased self-confidence and increased fear. Personal strengths and resilience can be forgotten when enduring these very difficult experiences. It is important when recovering from such experiences to rebuild a healthy identity by remembering personal strengths, regaining confidence, and re-establishing goals for the future. It is important not only to get through the period of crisis or illness but also to enjoy living life and enjoy being yourself again.

- **Reminding yourself of your interests**
  In order to maintain well-being it is important to be involved in activities that are stimulating to you. If you are unsure of your interests then it is important to spend time investigating and researching possibilities.

- **Eliminating unhelpful myths**
  Overly negative, unrealistic thoughts can cause difficulties in maintaining well-being. It is important to notice when you are experiencing these thoughts and transform them into more helpful thoughts. Some examples are listed below.

  "I should sacrifice my own needs for others." ⇒ "It is important to meet my own needs, and this will mean that I can be more helpful to others."

  "I must be really hopeless if I can't cope with this by myself." ⇒ "It is sign of strength and wisdom to notice when I need assistance and can skillfully access help."

  "If I experience difficult emotions I might lose control." ⇒ "Strong emotions are a natural experience; I can learn and use strategies to manage my difficult emotions."

- **Knowing your strengths as well as weaknesses**
  Difficult experiences can help you get to know yourself better, and this can be a great advantage. Remind yourself of the things that you are good at, and remember to keep doing them. Also take notice of things that you would like to improve and plan to get assistance with them. Also, learn to accept compliments from others.

- **Both accepting yourself as you are and accepting the need to change**
  It is important to be able to accept yourself with all your strengths and weaknesses and, at the same time, if problematic behaviours are present, to accept the need to change. It is unhelpful and unrealistic to pursue perfection and to be judgemental about weaknesses and problems as this can interfere with making plans to change.

- **Identify your own values and act in accordance with them**
  Understanding what is most important to you and making choices and decisions in line with these values fosters a sense of self-respect and focus that can help prevent recurrences of extreme stress.

- **Identify goals and plan to achieve them**
  During times of stress, future goals are often put to one side. It might be time to revisit or revise your goals and plan to take steps towards achieving them. These may be to develop interests and skills, to improve your lifestyle or take a holiday, to develop relationships, or work towards career or financial goals.

Handout 9.6   Page 2 of 2

Anger: how is it helpful and unhelpful?

Positive functions of anger:

- **Provides energy and motivation**: Anger provides more energy, motivation, and stamina to act and deal with conflict. You can use anger to your advantage by taking effective action.

- **Expression of tension**: Anger allows you to express tension and communicate negative feelings to others both nonverbally and verbally. It can prompt you to express your feelings to others and prevent tension from building up inside you.

- **Gives you information:** It is a signal that something is a problem either in a situation or within yourself or both. Anger can be an alerting signal that you are becoming upset, that it is a time to deal with stress.

- **Sense of control**: Anger can give you a sense of being in control and taking charge of a situation.

Problematic aspects of anger:

- **Stops you from thinking, feeling, and acting clearly**: When experiencing high levels of anger it is difficult to think clearly. This can lead to feeling out of control, to impulsive or risk-taking behaviour, and acting in ways that we later regret.

- **Too often and too intense**: High levels of anger put stress and strain on your body which can impact on your health. It is also likely that frequent or intense anger means that others may not enjoy their relationships with you.

- **Can lead to violence**: Anger can lead to aggression and violence, creating more relationship problems and legal problems. This has the potential to affect all aspects of your life, such as work, family, and freedom.

The triggers and consequences of anger

Listed below are the triggers and consequences of anger. As you can see, anger has consequences for both the individual (thoughts, feelings, and behaviours) who experiences it and for others who witness these effects. Add your own personal experiences related to anger to the list. Place a '✓' next to the ones you can relate to.

Triggers for anger	Thoughts when angry	Feelings when angry	Behaviours when angry	Consequences of anger
❑ Lack of respect	❑ "You're all bastards"	❑ Powerful	❑ Hyperventilate	❑ Deep sadness
❑ Lack of communication	❑ "Screw this world"	❑ Out of control	❑ Clench teeth	❑ Feared by others
❑ Lack of understanding	❑ "I just want to punch something"	❑ Ashamed	❑ Face gets red	❑ Loss of friends
❑ Memories of what others have done	❑ "This shouldn't be happening"	❑ Powerless	❑ Hit people	❑ Jail
❑ People yelling	❑ "Why am I here again?"	❑ Aggressive	❑ Keep it inside	❑ People think you are mad
❑ Abuse	❑ "I feel guilty"	❑ Anxious	❑ Cursing	❑ Hospitalisation
❑ Loneliness	❑ "I feel ashamed"	❑ Tense	❑ Trash furniture	❑ Aggression by others
❑ Bossiness	❑ "Everyone's out to get me!"	❑ Tightness	❑ Yelling	❑ Affects relationships
❑ Being forced to do something		❑	❑ Silence	❑
❑ Drugs and alcohol		❑	❑ Pull hair out	❑
❑ Lack of sleep		❑	❑ Take drugs	❑
		❑	❑	❑
		❑	❑	❑
		❑	❑	❑
		❑		❑

What can we do to change our experience of anger?

There are several stages when strategies can be implemented to improve our experience of anger.

The situation

- Avoid the situation or person.
- Remove yourself from the situation.
- Take time out from the situation.
- Distract yourself from the situation by doing or thinking about something else.

Thoughts

Challenge angry thoughts by considering:

- How bad is it really? (on a scale of 1 to 10)
- Does it really matter? Does it really change anything?
- What might be the other person's perspective?
- What will be the consequences to my well-being, my happiness, my family, and friends, if I act aggressively?
- What things am I in control of and what things am I not in control of?

Physical reaction

- Do something that relaxes you.
- Listen to relaxing music.
- Do some relaxation exercises.
- Go for a walk somewhere pleasant or quiet.

Behaviour response

- Get away from the situation—think about it and decide what the best thing for you to do is.
- Do some physical exercise.
- Talk to a friend and tell them how you feel.
- Write down how you feel.

Treating Stress and Anxiety © 2008 Crown House Publishing and Dr Lillian Nejad and Katerina Volny

Communication styles

Communication styles impact on our relationships and our progress towards our goals. It is important to identify when we may be communicating ineffectively and to know how to implement assertive communication.

1. **Passive or submissive:** Being passive or submissive involves not letting people know how you feel, what you think, and what you want. You might find yourself always going along with what others want and when asked for your opinion telling others that you don't care or that it doesn't matter to you. Often people who are passive can be described as "people-pleasers" or wanting to gain approval from others and not "rock the boat". You probably avoid conflict at all costs. Although being passive can sometimes be beneficial—for instance, when you encounter aggressive people, a passive stance can help prevent the situation from escalating and can help keep you safe—if you use this communication style all the time you are likely to eventually feel sad or resentful that your needs are never noticed or met.

2. **Aggressive:** Some people do not realise when they are communicating in an aggressive way. If you try to get what you want or need by intimidating others either by what you say or how you say it (tone of voice, stance, facial expression), or you don't pay attention or care how others feel or how others are responding to you as long as you get what you want, you have an aggressive communication style. Although being aggressive can sometimes be of benefit in that you achieve your goal of getting what you want, you are likely to be damaging your relationships with others as well as your self-respect.

3. **Passive–aggressive:** Sometimes people who are uncomfortable expressing their anger or frustration will communicate these feelings in an indirect or passive way. For example, if you are irritated that you have been asked to go grocery shopping you may express this by forgetting several important items on the list. Being passive–aggressive may make you feel satisfied in the short term but it does not enable you to learn how to get what you want or express your feelings in an effective way. This communication style may also alienate you from others who may not understand why you behave a certain way.

4. **Manipulative:** Being manipulative is trying to control a situation or get your needs met by making people feel guilty or sorry for you. This style can often be effective in the short term as people may initially respond in a caring and compassionate way; however, in the long term your relationships are likely to suffer. People may grow tired of feeling obligated to meet your needs and then become indifferent or resentful towards you.

5. **Assertive:** Assertive communication is effective in both getting your needs met as well as maintaining your relationships and self-respect. It involves directly, honestly, and appropriately expressing your feelings and what you want or

need. This includes saying no rather than always aiming to please others and standing up for yourself when others are disrespectful towards you.

Planning to communicate assertively

If these behaviours are not familiar to you, you are likely to require some practice and coaching before trying this in an important situation. Practising your assertive response with a friend or therapist is a helpful first step.

- Consider your rights in the situation.
- Consider your wants, your needs, and your feelings in the situation.
- Let go of blame, self-pity, and hurt.
- Define your goal and keep it in mind throughout the interaction.
- Arrange a time and a place to discuss your problem with the other person.
- Define the problem situation as specifically as possible.
- Describe your feelings without evaluation or blaming others, say "I feel ... when ..." rather than "You make me feel ..." Don't use generalisations such as "You always ..."
- Express your request in one or two easy to understand sentences. Be specific, act confident, and firm.
- Let the other person know the positive consequences of getting what you want.
- Use assertive body language by making and maintaining eye contact, having a confident but non-threatening posture, and speaking clearly.
- If you don't get the desired response at first, be persistent, be willing to negotiate, and try again. Note that no matter how skilled you are in communicating you will not always get the response that you want. Remember that expressing yourself effectively is the main goal and this will usually result in a positive interaction.

Handout 9.10   Page 2 of 2

Treating Stress and Anxiety © 2008 Crown House Publishing and Dr Lillian Nejad and Katerina Volny

Chapter 10

Group programmes to reduce anxiety and enhance well-being

There are many advantages to running groups for both clients and therapists. Unfortunately, any mention of joining a group programme can send clients running for cover. Groups often bring to mind a circle of people gathering to divulge their problems to perfect strangers and that is very daunting to the average person. Therapists may also find the thought of developing and facilitating a group too challenging or time-consuming. This chapter aims to highlight the many advantages of group programmes as well as acknowledge some of the common challenges that both therapists and clients face in a group situation. The structure and content of two group programmes—Enhancing Well-Being and Managing Anxiety and Panic—are also outlined for therapists to utilise in their own practice.

So what are the advantages of group programmes? Firstly, there are the practical considerations. In your assessment, you will find that some clients may be more suited to a group environment, others may benefit from attending both individual therapy and a group, and others may benefit most from individual attention. If you are able to offer both individual therapy and group programmes you provide your clients with more options. Furthermore, groups can be utilised in a therapeutic sense. For instance, groups can be a familiarisation process for clients who are uncertain about individual therapy or psychological assistance. They can also serve as an exposure exercise or as a way of increasing social interaction for clients that you are already seeing individually. Groups are also a cost-effective option for clients who cannot afford individual therapy and a time-efficient option for therapists who have long waiting lists. The message here is that group programmes are a great addition to any therapist's skill-set and practice, even if just in a practical sense. However, there are many other advantages to consider.

Group programmes have a number of benefits for clients. Groups provide a socialisation opportunity and a chance to meet new people with at least one goal in common. Interacting with others who have had similar struggles or experiences assists people in understanding that they are not alone. Seeing others in a group also normalises obtaining help and support. Furthermore, group members all have their own skills and strengths which they can impart and model for others. Both therapists and other group members can model adaptive, effective behaviours to others with specific skills deficits, like being able to communicate openly with others or being able to respectfully manage inappropriate or challenging behaviour. Groups, as opposed to individual counselling situations, give people the opportunity to receive feedback from a variety of individuals from diverse backgrounds and cultures and a range of expertise who can offer suggestions based on their own experiences. Groups can also foster positive peer pressure by encouraging all members to participate, to challenge themselves, and to complete homework. Offering support to others and participating in group activities and discussions can give group members a sense of mastery and provides at least one example of their ability to face their fears.

Groups also have their own set of challenges. The first one is convincing people that a group would be of benefit. Clients, especially anxious ones, and particularly socially anxious ones, will often baulk at the thought of joining a group. It is helpful to gain an understanding of their preconceived notions of what group programmes entail or what their past experiences have been. Then, explain the nature and purpose of the kind of group programme you are recommending and why you think it would be of benefit.

The groups outlined in this chapter are not "therapy" groups where participants spend a great deal of time working through their own personal issues. Rather, they are based on cognitive behavioural principles and designed to increase knowledge and impart relevant strategies and skills to help reduce anxiety and panic and to enhance well-being. With the focus on learning and practising skills, the group programmes are, in effect, much like a course or a class rather than a therapy group, although they do have therapeutic benefits. If, in your clinical judgement, your client would benefit from such a group, either run by you or other clinicians:

1. Predict and normalise their reservations, e.g., "I think a group would be really helpful for you. Often people feel really uncomfortable and anxious about joining a group. Is that how you feel? It's normal to feel a little anxious—even the facilitators feel anxious before a group. People usually think that they are going to have to talk in detail about their problems or hear about others' problems. The kind of group I'm talking about is …"
2. Spend time discussing the advantages and disadvantages of joining the group, e.g., a pros and cons list.
3. Highlight the advantages, particularly how it will help them achieve their goals.
4. Discuss ways of removing the barriers: breathing techniques, coping statements.
5. Give them time to think about it and make their own decision. Because groups require participation during the session as well as practice

in-between sessions it is important for prospective group members to be sufficiently motivated and committed to joining the group.

Considerations for facilitators

Below are some common barriers and difficulties faced by potential facilitators.

I don't have enough time; it's too much work

It is highly recommended that two therapists facilitate a group. This has several practical implications: (1) it splits the workload before, during, and after the group; (2) it allows for one of you to be sick and not cancel the group; (3) it is helpful if you have a situation that requires one of you to leave the group, e.g., if a client leaves in the middle of a session without saying anything one of you can find out what has happened; (4) it gives you a chance to discuss what went well and what could be improved after each session; and (5) you and your co-facilitator will have different skills, strengths, and experiences that will enrich the group.

I've never done this before; I feel anxious

Even the most experienced group facilitators feel anxious before starting a new group or session. After all, it's a form of public speaking, one of the most anxiety-provoking and feared situations that we can experience. What can be really useful for first-time facilitators is to pair yourself with a more experienced facilitator. If both of you are running a group for the first time, or running an anxiety/stress group for the first time, it is also helpful to be open about this to the potential participants. Let them know that this will also be a learning experience for you and that you will value their feedback at the end of the group. Being open about feeling a little anxious is also wonderfully normalising for group members. Also, see Chapters 1 to 7 for other ways to manage your anxiety.

Not enough time to cover everything

You will never be able to cover everything that you want and sometimes you will not cover everything that you planned. At the end of the group programme, distribute relevant articles and a list of related books, articles, and websites, as well as a list of local community resources that may be able to continue to provide support, groups, classes, or individual counselling. If you believe that group members would benefit from further individual psychological assistance, speak to them individually about their options.

Some group members can be over-talkative or otherwise inappropriate

There is often one person in a group who will be overly talkative or who will want to discuss their personal issues in detail or offer advice or be otherwise disruptive to the group process. Preventative measures are recommended by first having a pre-group assessment session with all prospective clients and, second, by discussing the group rules or agreement at the commencement of the group programme. A pre-group assessment may seem unnecessary and time-consuming; however, it has several functions. It assists facilitators in ascertaining whether the client's expectations match the group aims and to refer on if appropriate, whether the client's level of anxiety is too severe for a group setting, and whether the client has co-morbid issues that require intervention before joining the group (anxiety and depression issues, suicidal thoughts/behaviour). It is also a chance to introduce and discuss the group agreement. Prospective clients also benefit from a preliminary meeting as it provides them with a chance to meet the facilitators and helps them feel more comfortable and less anxious about coming to the first session.

At the beginning of the first session, introduce the group agreement and ask for the group's suggestions to add to the list. If someone does disrupt the group in any way, manage it immediately by respectfully reminding the person of the group agreement. See Handout 10.1 for a sample group agreement. Give each person a copy of the agreement and post it on a wall in the group room in case you need to refer to it. Note that part of the agreement is that facilitators can interrupt group members; this allows you to manage inappropriate behaviours more easily.

Examples:

> "Sally, I'm going to have to interrupt you now because we have to move on if we're going to cover everything."

> "I'm sorry, Robert, but we can't focus on the details of what happened to you during the week because of the time. Can you tell me what coping strategy you used?"

Helpful pre-group assessment questions

- What interests you about this group? What are your expectations of the group?
- This group is not a therapy group where you will have a chance to discuss your personal issues in detail, rather the focus is on learning and practising strategies that help manage stress and anxiety. There will also be homework in-between sessions. Do you think this fits with what you are wanting?
- How does anxiety/stress affect you and what are your current ways of coping?
- What other help have you sought (individual counselling, medication, other groups)? What was helpful or unhelpful?
- Is alcohol or drug use a current issue in your life?
- Do you experience suicidal thoughts or engage in self-harm behaviour?
- Do you have any other concerns or questions?

Other helpful tips regarding group structure, content and materials

Group structure

- Aim for a group of ten to twelve people. Keep in mind that no matter how well you assess people before the group and how committed people say they are you can count on one or two drop-outs. Therefore, accept twelve people into the group if you are aiming for a ten-person group.
- You need at least eight group sessions to see change. Both groups that are outlined in this chapter are eight sessions but can easily be modified and extended to ten or twelve sessions.
- Group sessions are generally one-and-half to two-and-half hours in length with a ten to twenty minute break in-between to allow for socialisation processes. The break also gives the facilitators time to prepare for the next section and to follow up with non-attendees, if necessary.
- Don't start the group too early in the morning or too late in the afternoon.
- Consider providing a follow-up "booster" or "trouble-shooting" session after one month to assess group members' continued practice of skills and to give them an opportunity to discuss difficulties. This is also a follow-up evaluation opportunity to assess maintenance of progress.
- Be mindful of public holidays and school holidays when scheduling groups.

Group content

- Use a variety of didactic (handouts, discussion, videos) and experiential (games, role-playing, relaxation exercises) methods to convey information and promote learning.
- Be flexible and adaptable with the group content to correspond to the needs of the group. For instance, if the majority of participants present with a similar issue that was not going to be covered in the group, like dealing with grief, adapt the group to incorporate discussion of this during the course.
- Provide relaxation exercise CDs or tapes to participants so they can practise in-between sessions.
- During relaxation exercises, post signs outside the room so that other distractions are kept to a minimum.
- Evaluate the group, preferably with both objective and subjective measures. You can evaluate progress and impact by using a validated anxiety or stress measure, as well as subjective mood ratings, practice charts, and confidence in using the strategies ratings (see Worksheets 10.1 and 10.2 for the SMARTS Chart for Stress and SMART Chart for Anxiety to measure strategies and mood ratings). Evaluate satisfaction with the content and process of group by giving group members a questionnaire at the end (see Handout 10.2 for a sample evaluation questionnaire).
- Certificates of successful completion of the group are usually well received and give group members a sense of accomplishment and achievement.

Group materials

- Group room should be large enough for all group members to sit in a circle. It should have a whiteboard for writing on and have adequate temperature control.
- Folders for participants to contain the handout materials they will receive throughout the group.
- Copies of session handouts that are provided in this workbook.
- When you write on the whiteboard during group discussions, consider making it into a handout to give to participants at the next session.
- Relaxation CD (or scripts to read yourself) and CD player.
- Mats and/or comfortable chairs for relaxation sessions.
- Relaxation exercise CDs or tapes for participants so they can practise in-between sessions.
- Refreshments during the break.
- Pens.
- Whiteboard markers.
- Nametags for every session.

Reducing and managing anxiety and panic group session outline

Content	Handouts
Session 1: Orientation and psychoeducation • Introduction to group and facilitators • Group agreement • Warm-up exercise • Assessment for pre-group evaluation: anxiety measure and SMART chart • Effects of anxiety: write on whiteboard, separate cognitive, behavioural, emotional, and physical symptoms • Give out handout, can tick own personal symptoms BREAK • Rationale for breathing and relaxation exercises—discuss guidelines • Short breathing exercise • Homework: practise breathing exercise, tick personal symptoms on effects of anxiety handout, read handouts	HO 10.2 Group Agreement WS 10.2 SMART Chart HO 1.4 Effects of Anxiety HO 5.1 The Purpose of Relaxation Exercises HO 5.2 Guidelines for Relaxation CD Relaxation Techniques to Reduce Stress and Anxiety
Session 2: Anxiety and panic • Introduce new members and brief review of last session if necessary • Fill out SMART chart • Review of homework: did they do breathing exercise, why or why not? Troubleshoot what got in the way. Helpful or unhelpful? Emphasise importance of practice in learning new skills • What is the function of anxiety and why do panic attacks occur? BREAK • Cycle of panic and how to break the cycle • Relaxation session • Homework: practise breathing and relaxation exercises, write down what situations lead to anxiety, read handouts	HO 1.3 What is Anxiety? HO 3.1 Strategies that Enhance Well-being and Break the Cycle of Anxiety and Panic

Content	Handouts
Session 3: Introduction to cognitive behavioural strategies	HO 6.1 Thoughts, Emotions and Behaviour: How They Work Together
• Brief review of last session	
• Fill out SMART chart	
• Review of homework: practised relaxation? Helpful/unhelpful? Write on whiteboard situations that trigger anxiety	HO 6.3 Tips to Manage Worrying
• Discussion of CBT model of anxiety with emphasis on the impact of thoughts on emotions and behaviour. Use example of situation from homework to illustrate	HO 6.4 More Strategies for Managing Persistent Unhelpful Thoughts
BREAK	HO 6.5 Affirmations
• Small group discussion—break up into pairs, talk about current coping strategies, then feedback to group—write on whiteboard	
• Introduce basic cognitive and behavioural coping strategies. Go over handouts: Tips to Manage Worrying and More Strategies for Managing Persistent Unhelpful Thoughts	
• Relaxation exercise	
• Homework: relaxation, practise one new behavioural and one new cognitive coping strategy, read handouts	
Session 4: Awareness of and challenging unhelpful thoughts	WS 6.1 Detecting Unhelpful Thoughts
• Brief review of last session	
• Fill out SMART chart	HO 6.2 Challenging Unhelpful Thoughts
• Review of homework: coping strategies. Helpful or unhelpful?	
• Review CBT model in terms of how thoughts affect emotions/behaviours	WS 6.2 Transforming Your Unhelpful Thoughts into Helpful Thoughts
• Discussion of common unhelpful thoughts. What sort of thoughts lead to stress? Which ones do you use most often? Write down examples of specific unhelpful thoughts on whiteboard	
BREAK	
• How do you detect and challenge unhelpful thoughts? Go over worksheet on Detecting Unhelpful Thoughts and handout on Challenging Unhelpful Thoughts	
• Small group activity. Each group of two or three discuss rebuttals of unhelpful thoughts: use examples given in previous discussion or use your own, then feedback to group—write on whiteboard	
• Relaxation exercise	
• Homework: relaxation, thought-monitoring and rebutting, read handouts	

Content	Handouts
Session 5: Introduction to graded exposure • Brief review of last session • Fill out SMART chart • Review of homework: what did you notice when you monitored your thoughts? Were you able to challenge your thoughts? Write up some examples on the board • Discussion of avoidance as common coping strategy for anxiety and need to face fears BREAK • Introduction to graded exposure: rationale and process • Whiteboard activity: situations that you avoid • Do an example of hierarchy for one situation • Relaxation exercise • Homework: relaxation, write down five situations that you avoid, rate from least feared to most feared situations, read handouts	HO 7.1 Why is it Important to Face Your fears? WS 7.1 Preparing to Face Your Fear
Session 6: Steps to facing fear • Brief review of last session • Fill out SMART chart • Review of homework: pick a situation that you would like to work on, suggest working on least feared to start • Ask for volunteer to talk about their feared situation and write down steps of hierarchy on whiteboard BREAK • Individual work on hierarchies, group leaders to assist • Review of exposure process, invite members to attempt first step on hierarchy for homework • Relaxation exercise • Homework: relaxation, continue to work on hierarchy for one situation and do first step if desired, read handouts	WS 7.2 Monitoring Your Fear

Content	Handouts
Session 7: Reducing vulnerability	HO 4.1 Emotional Health Check-up
• Brief review of last session	
• Fill out SMART chart	HO 4.2 Diet: Fuel for a Healthy Mind
• Review of homework: were there any difficulties with the hierarchies? Did anyone try the first step? What happened? How were you able to do it? Did you use any coping strategies before, during, and after? What stopped you from doing it? What might you need to do before you start?	HO 4.3 Exercise: The Great Mood Enhancer HO 4.4 Sleep Well
• Review everything covered in group so far, are there any questions?	WS 4.1 Sleep Diary
BREAK	
• Brainstorm factors that make people vulnerable to anxiety and panic, e.g. inadequate sleep and nutrition, lack of social supports, skills deficits (assertiveness, time management, etc.)	HO 4.5 Pleasant Activities WS 4.2 Activity Schedule
• Go over Emotional Check-up handout	
• Pairs discussion: what area needs the most attention? Go over handout for area that members indicate is most problematic, provide rest of handouts/worksheets at end of session	HO 4.6 Social Support WS 4.3 Time Management
• Relaxation exercise	WS 4.4 Problem Solving
• Homework: relaxation, read handouts, work on one area that makes you more vulnerable to anxiety and panic	

Content	Handouts
Session 8: Preventing and managing setbacks	HO 8.2 Preventing Relapse
• Brief review of last session	
• Fill out SMART chart: how have you progressed in practising skills and in level of anxiety over eight weeks. What has helped or been a barrier for you?	HO 8.1 List of Possible Triggers, Early Warning Signs and Strategies
• Review of homework: what areas did you work on? Discuss benefits and barriers	WS 8.1 Prevention Plan
• Discuss setbacks as part of the change process, importance not to label this as failure	Appendix B and C: list of references and websites for clients
• Go over relapse prevention handout	
BREAK	Provide list of community resources and agencies suitable for follow-up
• Strength card exercise: spread out notecards with "strengths" written on them (resourceful, energetic, creative) and ask group to pick out three that will help them manage their anxiety. Ask each individual to talk about what they chose and how it will help them	Provide certificates of completion
• Where to go from here: provide list of local resources for follow-up and a reference list	WS 10.2 SMART chart
• Evaluation: anxiety scale and group evaluation	HO 10.2 Evaluation of Group
• Finishing exercise: One thing that I will take from the group is ...	
• Handout certificates of completion	
• If follow-up group scheduled, remind group of time and date	
• Homework: continue practising strategies, fill out relapse prevention plan, hand out out new SMART chart so they can monitor progress	
Follow-up: Catching up and trouble-shooting	
• Informal discussion about how members are doing	
• Encourage practice of skills	
• Ask if there is anything they want to review	
• Review areas of interest	
• Group members participate in troubleshooting difficulties	
• Encourage getting appropriate follow-up if needed	
• Evaluation	

Enhancing well-being and reducing stress group outline

Content	Handouts
Session 1: Orientation and psychoeducation	HO 10.1 Group Agreement
• Introduction to group and facilitators	
• Group agreement	WS 10.1 SMARTS Chart
• Warm-up exercise	
• Assessment for pre-group evaluation: scales and SMARTS chart	HO 1.1 What is Stress?
• Psychoeducation about stress	HO 1.2 Effects of Stress
• Effects of stress: write on whiteboard, separate cognitive, behavioural, emotional, and physical symptoms	HO 5.1 Purpose of Relaxation Exercises
• Give out Effects of Stress handout	
BREAK	HO 5.2 Guidelines for Relaxation
• Discuss flight or fight response and rationale for breathing and relaxation exercises—go over guidelines	CD Relaxation Techniques to Reduce Stress and Anxiety
• Relaxation exercise	
• Homework: practise breathing exercise, tick personal symptoms on effects of anxiety handout, read handouts	
Session 2: Reducing vulnerability	HO 4.1 Emotional Health Check-up
• Introduce new members and brief review of last session if necessary	
• Fill out SMARTS chart	
• Review of homework: did they do relaxation exercise? Why or why not? Troubleshoot what got in the way. Helpful or unhelpful? Emphasise importance of practice in learning new skills	
• Brainstorm factors that make people vulnerable to stress, e.g. inadequate sleep and nutrition, lack of social supports, skills deficits (assertiveness, time management, etc.)	
BREAK	
• Go over Emotional Check-up handout	
• Pairs discussion: what area needs the most attention?	
• Discuss areas of vulnerability in pairs: what are the top three areas of concern? Will focus on these in following sessions (following three sessions may differ according to group's needs)	
• Relaxation exercise	
• Homework: relaxation, read handouts	

Content	Handouts
Session 3: Strategies to improve sleep	HO 4.4 Sleep Well
• Brief review of last session	
• Fill out SMARTS chart	WS 4.1 Sleep Diary
• Review of homework	
• Discussion of sleeping problems and their effects—particularly the link between stress and sleep	HO 6.3 Tips to Manage Worrying
• Go over Sleep Well handout	
BREAK	
• Continue to go over Sleep Well handout	
• Emphasise need to manage worries	
• Go over handout on Managing Worrying	
• Ask group members which two strategies they are going to try for homework	
• Relaxation exercise	
• Homework: relaxation, practise two strategies to manage sleep and worries, read handouts	
Session 4: Pleasant activities, time management and social support	HO 4.5 Pleasant Activities: A Life Worth Living
• Brief review of last session	
• Fill out SMARTS chart	WS 4.2 Activity Schedule
• Review of homework: strategies helpful or unhelpful?	WS 4.3 Time Management
• Discussion of the need to incorporate pleasant activities into daily life. Social activities part of this. Write down examples on whiteboard. What gets in the way? Often don't believe they deserve to take a break, waste of time, don't have the time	HO 4.6 Social Support
• Go over Time Management handout	
BREAK	
• Discuss importance of social support and contact. People becoming more isolated. Why is this? What are the barriers to socialising or getting support from others—discuss in pairs and then in group, write on whiteboard	
• Go over Social Support handout	
• Ask everyone to write down one pleasant activity they will do during the week and one social activity (even if making a phone call or a plan to go out)	
• Relaxation exercise	
• Homework: relaxation, pleasant and social activity, read handouts	

Content	Handouts
Session 5: Detecting and challenging unhelpful thoughts • Brief review of last session • Fill out SMARTS chart • Review of homework: were you able to do activities? Why or why not? What will help you do it this week? Try to increase activity this week • Describe CBT model in terms of how thoughts affect emotions/behaviours • Discussion of common unhelpful thoughts. What sort of thoughts lead to stress? Which ones do you use most often? Write down examples of specific unhelpful thoughts on whiteboard BREAK • How do you detect and challenge unhelpful thoughts? Go over worksheet on Detecting Unhelpful Thoughts and handout on Challenging Unhelpful Thoughts • Small group activity, each group of two or three discuss rebuttals of unhelpful thoughts: use examples given in previous discussion or use your own, then feedback to group—write on whiteboard • Go over handout: More Strategies for Managing Persistent Unhelpful Thoughts. Ask each person to pick out an affirmation to use during the week • Relaxation exercise • Homework: relaxation, thought-monitoring and rebutting, affirmations, read handouts	HO 6.1 Thoughts, Emotions, and Behaviour: How They Work Together WS 6.1 Detecting Unhelpful Thoughts HO 6.2 Challenging Unhelpful Thoughts WS 6.2 Transforming your Unhelpful Thoughts into Helpful Thoughts HO 6.4 More Strategies for Managing Persistent Unhelpful Thoughts HO 6.5 Affirmations

Content	Handouts
Session 6: More on thoughts and communication skills • Brief review of last session • Fill out SMARTS chart • Review of homework: Review of homework: what did you notice when you monitored your thoughts? Were you able to challenge your thoughts? Did you find affirmations useful? Why or why not? • Ask for volunteer to talk about their situation in detail: situation, emotions, thoughts, behaviours, and rebuttals. Ask for input from others BREAK • Discuss difficulties people have communicating: common problems include unable to assert self, difficulty saying no, wanting to avoid conflict at any cost • Go over communication skills handouts • Emphasise that no matter how skilful you are it doesn't ensure you will get the response you want. Also, that people may not react favourably to changes you make especially if you have been a "people pleaser" • Practise role-plays in small groups: practise broken record technique (how to say no) • Relaxation exercise • Homework: relaxation, continue to work on challenging thoughts and go over Communication Styles handout	HO 9.10 Communication Styles
Session 7: Strengthening identity • Brief review of last session • Fill out SMARTS chart • Review of homework • Review everything covered in group so far, are there any questions? • Strength card exercise: spread strength cards out and ask group to pick out three of their strengths (their own opinion, not others'). Discuss in pairs why they chose these strengths • Ask each individual to talk about one strength and why they chose it—point out how they can use this strength in managing stress and improving their quality of life BREAK • Go over handouts on Self-acceptance and Strengthening Identity • Relaxation exercise • Homework: relaxation, read handouts, work on one area that strengthens identity	HO 9.6 Self-acceptance and Strengthening Identity

Content	Handouts
Session 8: Effective problem solving and goal setting	WS 4.4 Problem Solving
• Brief review of last session	
• Fill out SMARTS chart: how have you progressed in practising skills and in level of stress over eight weeks? What has helped or been a barrier for you?	Appendix B and C: list of references and websites for clients
• Review of homework: what areas did you work on? Discuss benefits and barriers	Provide list of community resources and agencies suitable to follow-up
• Discuss importance of planning for the future and being able to find solutions to problems or barriers that arise	Provide certificates of completion
• Go over Problem Solving handout	WS 10.1 SMARTS chart
• Write example on whiteboard	
BREAK	HO 10.2 Evaluation of Group
• Goal-setting exercise: write down three goals, one short-term, one medium-term, and one long-term. How are you going to use what you have learned during this group to achieve your goals? Write down the steps needed to achieve the short-term goal. Group leaders to help individuals with this task	
• Where to go from here: provide list of local resources for follow-up and a reference list	
• Evaluation: scales (anxiety/depression) and group evaluation	
• Finishing exercise: one thing that I will take from the group is …	
• Hand out certificates of completion	
• If follow-up group scheduled, remind group of time and date	
• Homework: continue practising strategies, fill out steps to achieving your goals, hand out new SMARTS chart so they can monitor skills and progress	
Follow-up: catching up and troubleshooting	
• Informal discussion about how members are doing	
• Encourage practise of skills	
• Ask if there is anything they want to review	
• Review areas of interest	
• Group members participate in troubleshooting difficulties	
• Encourage getting appropriate follow-up if needed	
• Evaluation	

Group agreement

Information sharing and strategy-focused group

- Participation and practise is necessary in group and in-between sessions

- The group will start on time and finish on time

- Contact facilitators if unable to attend group

- Maintain confidentiality

- Be respectful of others (no judging or criticising)

- Rather than advice-giving, make suggestions based on own experiences using "I" statements

- Give group members a chance to share equally

- One person to speak at a time

- Give group members a chance to share equally

- Facilitators may interrupt others at times (to keep the group on track and for time purposes)

Any others?

Evaluation of group

We would appreciate your honest feedback as it will help guide how we run future groups. You do not have to include your name but you can if you want to. Thank you.

1. What has been helpful and what have you liked about the content (topics covered) and/or the process (how the group was structured and run) of the group?

   _____

   _____

   _____

2. What might you like to change or improve about the content or process of the group?

   _____

   _____

   _____

3. Please circle a number on the scale from 1 to 10 to indicate your level of satisfaction with the group:

1	2	3	4	5	6	7	8	9	10

Not at all satisfied	*Somewhat satisfied*	*Very satisfied*

4. Please rate how helpful you found the group:

1	2	3	4	5	6	7	8	9	10

Not at all helpful	*Somewhat helpful*	*Very helpful*

5. Please rate how confident you feel in being able to implement the strategies you learned in the group in the future:

1	2	3	4	5	6	7	8	9	10

Not at all confident	*Somewhat confident*	*Very confident*

Handout 10.2   Page 1 of 2

6. Please rate your overall satisfaction with the facilitators:

1	2	3	4	5	6	7	8	9	10

Not at   *Somewhat*   *Very*
all satisfied   *satisfied*   *satisfied*

7. Would you recommend this group to others: **YES**   **NO**
   Why or why not?

_____

_____

_____

8. Any other comments?

_____

_____

_____

_____

_____

_____

_____

Thank you

Handout 10.2   Page 2 of 2

"SMARTS" chart for stress

Instructions

Each week, rate how often you utilised each strategy to reduce stress on a scale from 1 (not at all) to 10 (every day or several times a day):

1	2	3	4	5	6	7	8	9	10
Not at all				Some days					Every day

Then rate your level of stress for the week on a scale from 1 (no stress) to 10 (extreme stress):

1	2	3	4	5	6	7	8	9	10
No stress				Moderate stress					Extreme stress

	Week 1	Week 2	Week 3	Week 4	Week 5	Week 6	Week 7	Week 8
Seek support								
Manage your time								
Assertively communicate								
Relax and have fun								
Take care of yourself								
Strengthen self-esteem								
Rate your level of stress								

Worksheet 10.1   Page 1 of 2

Every week, fill out the chart above as a way to monitor what strategies you are using to reduce and manage stress in your life. Rate how much attention you give to the five following strategies. You will be familiar with some of these strategies and not with others. The following provides a brief explanation of the strategies:

1. **S**eek social support: Strong social support is very important especially when you are feeling stressed. It's okay to ask for help. People you could contact are friends, family members, counsellors, GPs, psychiatrists—whoever you feel comfortable talking to.

2. **M**anage your time: People often feel overwhelmed by the things they have to do (see the Time Management worksheet).

3. **A**ssertively communicate: Many people become stressed because they are unable to communicate their needs and wants to others or they are always putting others' needs before their own. In order to manage stress effectively it is important to attend to your needs and wants. Assertiveness includes the ability to set limits for yourself and communicate them effectively with others, to say "no" when appropriate, and to respect yourself as well as others.

4. **R**elax and have fun: Relaxation includes any activity that calms the mind and body. Examples of relaxation activities are meditation, breathing and relaxation exercises, walking, listening to soothing music, swimming, taking a hot bath, getting a massage, sitting in a park, etc. These activities help reduce muscle tension and overall levels of stress and increase the "feel-good" chemicals in the body. It is also important to have fun! People often think that they don't have time for fun but it's important to work it into your schedule.

5. **T**ake care of yourself: Create a healthy lifestyle to both prevent and reduce stress. First, *eat mostly healthy foods*. Become more aware of what foods/drinks make you feel healthy and give you more energy and what foods/drinks zap your energy or affect your ability to relax. *Regular physical activity* is another way to reduce stress levels. If you are not used to being active, start slowly and gradually, plan a convenient time, and choose activities that you enjoy. Make sure you also have *adequate and restful sleep*. People often have difficulty sleeping when they're stressed which usually leads to feeling more stressed the next day. If you are having trouble sleeping, there are many non-medical strategies you can use to sleep well again (see the Sleep Well handout).

6. **S**trengthen self-esteem: Having a positive sense of self makes it easier for people to manage setbacks, learn from mistakes, communicate with others, and set realistic expectations. It is important to challenge and change self-critical and negative thoughts to more helpful and realistic ones to reduce stress. It can be useful to see a counsellor or psychologist to help you develop your self-esteem.

These are the strategies to be mindful of during the week. Just taking small steps in one or two areas may be very challenging for some of you, and others may be able to give some attention to all of these areas. Keep this handout somewhere visible in your home to remind you of these strategies during the week.

Worksheet 10.1   Page 2 of 2

"SMART" chart for anxiety and panic

Instructions

Each week, rate how often you utilised each strategy to reduce anxiety on a scale from 1 (not at all) to 10 (every day or several times a day):

1	2	3	4	5	6	7	8	9	10
Not at all				Some days					Every day

Then rate your level of anxiety for the week on a scale from 1 (no anxiety) to 10 (extreme anxiety):

1	2	3	4	5	6	7	8	9	10
No anxiety				Moderate anxiety					Extreme anxiety

	Week 1	Week 2	Week 3	Week 4	Week 5	Week 6	Week 7	Week 8
Self-care								
Manage panic symptoms								
Activities that promote relaxation								
Replace unhelpful thoughts								
Tackle your fears								
Rate your level of stress								

Worksheet 10.2   Page 1 of 2

164

Every week, fill out the chart above as a way to monitor what strategies you are using to manage anxiety and panic. Rate how much attention you give to five strategies: self-care, managing panic symptoms, activities that promote relaxation, replacing unhelpful thoughts, and tackling your fears. You will be familiar with some of these strategies and not with others. The following provides a brief explanation of the strategies:

1. **S**elf-care: Self-care is about making sure your basic needs are met. It is important not to neglect yourself. Taking care of yourself is one of the first things you can do to make yourself feel better. This means taking regular showers, keeping your house tidy, making sure you eat healthy meals, getting some exercise, and getting enough sleep.

2. **M**anage panic symptoms: There are several ways that you can manage the panic symptoms that you may experience (racing heart, sweating, choking feeling). These tools can be useful for preventing panic symptoms as well as coping during panic experiences. Strategies include breathing exercises, distraction, and thought-stopping. Refer to Handout 3.1 for descriptions of these strategies.

3. **A**ctivities that promote relaxation: Activities that promote relaxation are important for lowering your general level of stress and tension and include any activity that calms the mind and body. Examples of beneficial activities are meditation, relaxation exercises, walking, listening to soothing music, swimming, taking a hot bath, getting a massage, sitting in a park, etc.

4. **R**eplace unhelpful thoughts: When people are anxious, they often think negative thoughts that are sometimes unrealistic or overly critical. Panic also creates a cycle of fear that is maintained by thoughts like "What if …" or "I must be going crazy." It is important to challenge these thoughts and change them to more helpful and realistic statements which help reduce fear, anxiety, and panic. Coping statements can replace negative thoughts or worries. Examples of coping statements are: "I will be okay," "I can cope with this," and "I have been able to do this in the past." Choose one or two statements for yourself to replace negative self-talk when you are experiencing anxiety symptoms.

5. **T**ackle your fears: "Doing" is an important part of reducing fear and anxiety. People often avoid activities or situations that they find anxiety-provoking. While this reduces anxiety in the short term, it increases fear and anxiety of the situation in the long term. In short, avoidance breeds fear. It is important to set realistic goals to face feared situations a small step at a time. Small steps and repeated practice in the feared situations help to eventually reduce anxiety and panic symptoms associated with these situations. Expect to feel uncomfortable when taking these steps. You can use the above strategies (relaxation, coping statements) to manage your discomfort.

These are the strategies to be mindful of during the week. Just taking small steps in one or two areas may be very challenging for some of you and others may be able to give some attention to all of these areas.

Worksheet 10.2 Page 2 of 2

Appendix A

Recommended reading for clinicians

American Psychiatric Association (1998). *Practice Guideline for the Treatment of Patients with Panic Disorder*. Washington, DC: American Psychiatric Association.

American Psychological Association. (2000). *Diagnostic and Statistical Manual of Mental Disorders* (4th edn rev.). Washington, DC: American Psychological Association.

Beck, A. T. (1975) *Cognitive Therapy and the Emotional Disorders*. New York: International Universities Press Inc.

Beck, A. T., Emery, G., & Greenberg, R. (1985). *Anxiety Disorders and Phobias: A Cognitive Perspective*. New York: Basic Books.

Beck, J. S. (1995). *Cognitive Therapy: Basics and Beyond*. New York: Guilford Press.

Beckham, E., & Leber, W. (eds.) (1995). *Handbook of Depression* (2nd edn). New York: Guilford Press.

Benson, H., & Klipper, M. Z. (1975, repr. 2000). *The Relaxation Response*. New York: Marrow.

Blume, A. W. (2005). *Treating Drug Problems*. Hoboken, NJ: John Wiley.

Brantley, J., & Kabat-Zinn, J. (2003) *Calming Your Anxious Mind: How Mindfulness and Compassion Can Free You from Anxiety and Panic*. Oakland, CA: New Harbinger Publications Inc.

Craske M. G., & Barlow D. H. (1990). *Therapist's Guide for the Mastery of Your Anxiety and Panic (MAP) Program*. Albany, NY: Graywind Publishing Co.

Creamer, M., Forbes, D., Phelps, A., & Humphrey, L. (2004). *Treating Traumatic Stress: Conducting Imaginal Exposure in PTSD*. Australian Centre for Posttraumatic Mental Health: University of Melbourne.

Crozier, W. R., & Alden, L. E. (eds.) (2005). *Essential Handbook of Social Anxiety for Clinicians*. Chichester: John Wiley.

Ellis, A., Harper, R. A., & Powers, M. (1975) *A Guide to Rational Living*. Hollywood, CA: Wiltshire Book Company.

Hawton, K., Salkovskis, P. M., Kirk, J., & Clark, D. (1989). *Cognitive Behaviour Therapy for Psychiatric Problems: A Practical Guide*. Oxford: Oxford University Press.

Hunter, M. (2007) *Healing Scripts: Using Hypnosis to Treat Trauma and Stress*. Carmarthen: Crown House Publishing.

Leahy, R. L., & Holland, S. J. (2000). *Treatment Plans and Interventions for Depression and Anxiety Disorders.* New York: Guilford Press.

Linehan, M. (1993). *Skills Training Manual for Treating Borderline Personality Disorder.* New York: Guilford Press.

Menzies, R. G., & de Silva, P. (eds.) (2003). *Obsessive-Compulsive Disorder: Theory, Research and Treatment*. Chichester: John Wiley

Nathan, P., & Gorman, J. (eds.) (1997). *A Guide to Treatments That Work*. New York: Oxford University Press.

Segal, Z. V., Williams, M. G., & Teasdale, J. D. (2002) *Mindfulness-based Cognitive Therapy for Depression: A New Approach to Preventing Relapse*. New York: Guilford Press.

Wilson, R. R. (2003). *Facing Panic: Self-help for People With Panic Attacks*. Silver Spring, MD: ADAA.

Appendix B

Recommended reading for clients

Panic and anxiety

Bourne, E. J. (2005). *The Anxiety and Phobia Workbook*. Oakland, CA: New Harbinger Publications, Inc.

Brantley, J., & Kabat-Zinn, J. (2003) *Calming Your Anxious Mind: How Mindfulness and Compassion Can Free You from Anxiety and Panic*. Oakland, CA: New Harbinger Publications, Inc.

Craske, M. G., & Barlow, D. H. (1994). *Agoraphobia Supplement to Mastery of Your Anxiety and Panic* (2nd edn). San Antonio, TX: Psychological Corp., Harcourt Brace & Co.

Craske, M. G., Meadows, E., & Barlow, D. H. (1994). *Mastery of Your Anxiety and Panic* (2nd edn). San Antonio, TX: Psychological Corp., Harcourt Brace & Co.

Foa, E. B., & Wilson, R. R. (2001). *Stop Obsessing*. New York: Bantam Books.

Martin, A., & Swinson, R. (2000). *The Shyness and Social Anxiety Workbook: Proven Techniques for Overcoming Your Fears*. Oakland, CA: New Harbinger Publications, Inc.

Smith, L. L., & Elliot, C. H. (2003). *Overcoming Anxiety for Dummies*. New York: John Wiley Publishing, Inc.

Wilson, R. R. (1996). *Don't Panic: Taking Control of Anxiety Attacks*. New York: Harper Perennial.

Wilson, R. R. (2003). *Facing Panic: Self-help for People with Panic Attacks*. Silver Spring, MD: ADAA.

Stress and relaxation

Benson, H., & Klipper, M. Z. (1975). *The Relaxation Response*. New York: Morrow.

Davis, M., Eshelman, E. R., & McKay, M. (1995). *The Relaxation and Stress Reduction Workbook*. New York: MJF Books.

Kabat-Zinn, J. (1990) *Full Catastrophe Living: Using the Wisdom of Your Body and Mind to Face Stress, Pain and Illness*. New York: Dell Publishing.

Walker, E. (2000). *Learn to Relax: Proven Techniques for Reducing Stress, Tension and Anxiety—and Promoting Peak Performance*. New York: John Wiley & Sons, Inc.

Depression and self-esteem

Burns, D. (1999). *Feeling Good: The New Mood Therapy* (rev. edn). New York: Avon.

Copeland, M. (2002). *The Depression Workbook: A Guide to Living with Depression and Manic Depression.* (2nd edn). Oakland, CA: New Harbinger Publications, Inc.

McKay, M., & Fanning, P. (2000). *Self-esteem* (3rd edn). Oakland, CA: New Harbinger Publications, Inc.

Yapko, M. (1997). *Breaking the Patterns of Depression.* New York: Doubleday.

General mental health

Bloch, D. (1990). *Words That Heal: Affirmations and Meditations For Daily Living.* New York: Bantam.

Ellis, A. (2001). *Feeling Better, Getting Better, Staying Better: Profound Self-Help Therapy for Your Emotions.* Atascedero: Impact Publishers.

McKay, D., Davis, M., Fanning, P., & McKay, M. (1997). *How to Communicate: The Ultimate Guide to Improving Your Personal and Professional Relationships.* MJF Books.

Prochaska, J., Norcross, J., & DiClemente, C. (1994). *Changing For Good: The Revolutionary Program That Explains the Six Changes of Change and Teaches You How to Free Yourself From Bad Habits.* New York: William Morrow & Co., Inc.

Shatte, A., & Reivich, K. (2003). *The Resilience Factor: 7 Essential Skills for Overcoming Life's Inevitable Obstacles.* New York, NY: Broadway Books.

Appendix C

Recommended websites for clinicians and clients

www.anxieties.com
A free self-help programme for anxiety

www.nimh.nih.gov
National Institute of Mental Health website which contains all the latest on mental health research and educational materials on anxiety and other mental health issues

www.ahrq.gov
The Agency of Healthcare Research and Quality

www.ocdfoundation.org
Information about obsessive compulsive disorder and interactive areas

www.moodgym.anu.edu.au
A self-help programme for depression and anxiety based on cognitive behavioural techniques

www.sane.org (click on 'StigmaWatch)
SANE provides advocacy, education, and research on mental health issues including a StigmaWatch programme and factsheets for consumers, carers, and the public

www.webmd.com
Provides information about physical and mental health issues

www.nami.org
The National Alliance on Mental Illness is an advocacy organisation for consumers and carers affected by mental health issues

www.adaa.org
The Anxiety Disorders Association of America provides resources and information about anxiety disorders

www.ahrq.gov
The Agency of Healthcare Research and Quality provides clinical information and research findings for clinicians and consumers

www.mentalhealthamerica.net
Formerly known as the National Mental Health Association, this organisation provides advocacy, education, research, and referral for people with mental health issues, their families, and the general public

www.hsph.harvard.edu/nutritionsource
The Harvard School of Public Health provides information about nutrition guidelines based on the latest research

References

American Psychological Association (2000). *Diagnostic and Statistical Manual of Mental Disorders* (4th edn rev.). Washington, DC: American Psychological Association.

Andrews, G., Hall, W., Teesson, M., & Henderson, S. (1999). *The Mental Health of Australians. National Survey of Mental Health and Wellbeing. National Mental Health Strategy*. Canberra: Commonwealth Department of Health and Aged Care.

Australian Bureau of Statistics (1997). *National Survey of Mental Health and Wellbeing of Adults*. Canberra: Australian Bureau of Statistics.

Baer, R. A. (2003). Mindfulness training as a clinical intervention: a conceptual and empirical review. *Clinical Psychology: Science and Practice*, 10(2), 125–143.

Ballenger, J. C. (2001). Overview of different pharmacotherapies for attaining remission in generalized anxiety disorder. *Journal of Clinical Psychiatry*, 62, 11–19.

Ballenger, J. C., Davidson, J. R., LeCrubier, Y., Nutt, D. J., Baldwin, D. S., Denboer, J. A., Kasper, S., & Shear, M. K. (1998). Consensus statement on panic disorder from the International Consensus Group on Depression and Anxiety. *Journal of Clinical Psychiatry*, 59, 47–54.

Barlow, D. H., O'Brien, G. T., & Last, C. G. (1984). Couples treatment of agoraphobia. *Behavior Therapy*, 15, 41–59.

Beck, A. T. (1975) *Cognitive Therapy and the Emotional Disorders*. New York: International Universities Press Inc.

Beck, A. T., Emery, G., & Greenberg, R. (1985). *Anxiety Disorders and Phobias: A Cognitive Perspective*. Basic Books: New York.

Beck, A. T., Epstein, N., Brown, G., & Steer, R. A. (1988). An inventory for measuring clinical anxiety: psychometric properties. *Journal of Consulting and Clinical Psychology*, 56, 893–7.

Beck, A. T., Ward, C. H., Mendelson, M., Mock, J. E., & Erbaugh, J. K. (1961). An inventory for measuring depression. *Archives of General Psychiatry*, 33, 561–71.

Benson, Herbert (1975). *The Relaxation Response*. New York: Morrow,

Bourne, Edmund (1995). The *Anxiety and Phobia Workbook*. Oakland, CA: New Harbinger Publications, Inc.

Brady, K., Pearlstein, T., Asnis, G. M., Baker, D., Rothbaum, B., Sikes, C. R., & Farfel, G. M. (2000). Efficacy and safety of sertraline treatment of posttraumatic stress disorder: a randomized controlled trial. *JAMA*, 283(14),1837–44.

Brantley, J., & Kabat-Zinn, J. (2003) *Calming Your Anxious Mind: How Mindfulness and Compassion Can Free You from Anxiety and Panic*. Oakland, CA: New Harbinger Publications, Inc.

Brown, T. A., Antony, M. M., & Barlow, D. H. (1995). Diagnostic comorbidity in panic disorder: effect on treatment outcome and course of comorbid diagnoses following treatment. *Journal of Consulting and Clinical Psychology*, 63, 408–18.

Brown, T. A., & Barlow, D. H. (1992). Comorbidity among anxiety disorders: implications for treatment and DSM-IV. *Journal of Consulting and Clinical Psychology*, 60(6), 835–44.

Bruce, T. J., & Saeed, S. A. (1999). Social anxiety disorder: a common, underrecognized mental disorder. *American Family Physician*, 60(8), 2311–20.

Brunello, N., Davidson, J. R., Deahl, M., Kessler, R. C., Mendlewicz, J., Racagni, G., Shalev, A. Y., & Zohar, J. (2001). Posttraumatic stress disorder: diagnosis and epidemiology, comorbidity and social consequences, biology and treatment. *Neuropsychobiology*, 43(3), 150–62.

Brunello, N., den Boer, J. A., Judd, L. L., Kasper, S., Kelsey, J. E., Lader, M., Lecrubier, Y., Lepine, J. P., Lydiard, R. B., Mendlewicz, J., Montgomery, S. A., Racagni, G., Stein, M. B., & Wittchen, H. U. (2000). Social phobia: diagnosis and epidemiology, neurobiology and pharmacology, comorbidity and treatment. *Journal of Affective Disorders*, 60(1), 61–74.

Burbach, F. R. (1997). The efficacy of physical activity interventions within mental health services: anxiety and depressive disorders. *Journal of Mental Health*, 6(6), 543–66.

Cerny, J. A., Barlow, D. H., Craske, M. G., & Himadi, W. G. (1987). Couples treatment of agoraphobia: a two-year follow-up. *Behavior Therapy*, 18, 401–16.

Cox, B. J., Norton, G. R., Swinson, R. P., & Endler, N. S. (1990). Substance abuse and panic-related anxiety: a critical review. *Behaviour Research and Therapy*, 28, 385–93.

Craske, M. G., & Barlow, D. H. (1994) *Agrophobia Supplement to Mastery of Your Anxiety and Panic* (2nd edn). San Antonio, TX: Psychological Corp., Harcourt Brace & Co.

Curtis, G. C., Magee, W. J., Eaton, W. W., Wittchen, H. U., & Kessler, R. C. (1998). Specific fears and phobias: epidemiology and classification. *British Journal of Psychiatry*, 173, 212–17.

Davidson, J. R. (2000). Pharmacotherapy of posttraumatic stress disorder: treatment options, long-term follow-up, and predictors of outcome. *Journal of Clinical Psychiatry*, 61, 52–56.

Deberry, S. (1982). The effects of meditation-relaxation on anxiety and depression in a geriatric population. *Psychotherapy: Theory, Research, and Practice*, 19, 512–21.

Demyttenaere, K., Bruffaerts, R., Posada-Villa, J., Gasquet, I., Kovess, V., Lepine, J. P., Angermeyer, M. C., Bernert, S., de Birolamo, G., Morosini, P., Polidori, G., Kikkawa, T., Kawakami, N., Ono, Y., Takeshima, T., Uda, H., Karam, E. G., Fayyad, J. A., Karam, A. N., Mceimneh, Z. N., Medina-Mora, M. E., Borges, G., Lara, C., de Graaf, R., Ormel, J., Gureje, O., Shen, Y., Huang, Y., Zhang, M., Alonso, J., Haro, J. M., Vilagut, G., Bromet, E. J., Gluzman, S., Webb, C., Kessler, R. C., Merikangas, K. R., Anthony, J. C., Von Korff, M. R., Wang, P. S., Brugha, T. S., Aguilar-Gaxiola, S., Lee, S., Heeringa,

S., Pennell, B. E., Zaslavsky, A. M., Ustun, T. B. Chatterji, S., WHO World Mental Health Survey Consortium (2004). Prevalence, severity and unmet need for treatment of mental disorders in the World Health Organization World Mental Health Surveys. *Journal of the American Medical Association*, 291, 2581–90.

Derogatis, L. R. (1977). SCL-90: *Administration, Score and Procedure Manual—I for the R (Revised) Version*. Baltimore, MD: Johns Hopkins University School of Medicine.

DiNardo, P. A., & Barlow, D. H. (1988). *Anxiety Disorders Interview Schedule-Revised (ADIS-R)*. Albany, NY: Phobia and Anxiety Disorders Clinic.

Fals-Stewart, W., Marks, A. P., & Schafer, J. (1993). A comparison of behavioral group therapy and individual behavior therapy in treating obsessive–compulsive disorder. *Journal of Nervous and Mental Disease*, 181, 189–93.

Foa, E. B., Davidson, J. R. T., & Frances, A. (1999). Treatment of postraumatic stress disorder. *Journal of Clinical Psychiatry*, 60, (suppl. 16).

Foa, E. B., & Goldstein, A. (1978). Continuous exposure and complete response prevention in the treatment of obsessive–compulsive neurosis. *Behavior Therapy*, 9, 821–9.

Foa, E. B., Hearst-Ikeda, D., & Perry, K. J. (1995). Evaluation of a brief cognitive–behavioral program for the prevention of chronic PTSD in recent assault victims. *Journal of Consulting and Clinical Psychology*, 63, 948–55.

Foa, E. B., Liebowitz, M. R., Kozak, M. J., Davies, S., Campeas, R., Franklin, M. E., Huppert, J. D., Kjernisted, K., Rowan, V., Schmidt, A. B., Simpson, H. B., & Tu, X. (2005). Randomized, placebo-controlled trial of exposure and ritual prevention, clomipramine, and their combination in the treatment of obsessive–compulsive disorder. *American Journal of Psychiatry*, 162, 151–61.

Foa, E. B., Rothbaum, B. O., Riggs, D., & Murdock, T. B. (1991). Treatment of post-traumatic stress disorder in rape victims. *Journal of Consulting and Clinical Psychology*, 59, 715–23.

Foa, E. B., & Wilson, R. R. (2001). *Stop Obsessing: How To Overcome Your Obsessions and Compulsions*. New York: Bantam Books.

Goodman, W. K., Price, L. H., Rasmussen, S. A., Mazure, C., Fleischmann, R. L., Hill, C. L., Heninger, G. R., & Charney, D. S. (1989). The Yale-Brown Obsessive Compulsive Scale. *Archives of General Psychiatry*, 46, 1006–11.

Grant, B. F., Stinson, F. S., Dawson, D. A., Chou, S. P., Dufour, M. C., Compton, W., Pickering, R. P., & Kaplan, K. (2004). Prevalence and co-occurrence of substance use disorders and independent mood and anxiety disorders: results from the National Epidemiologic Survey on Alcohol and Related Conditions. *Archives of General Psychiatry*, 61(8), 807–16.

Greist, J. H., Jefferson, J. W., Kobak, K. A., Katzelnik, D. J., & Serlin, R. C. (1995). Efficacy and tolerability of serotonin transport inhibitors in obsessive–compulsive disorder: a meta-analysis. *Archives of General Psychiatry*, 52, 53–60.

Harvard School of Public Health (2007) *The Nutrition Source*. <www.hsph.harvard.edu/nutritionsource>

Hunter, M. E. (2007). *Healing Scripts: Using Hypnosis to Treat Trauma and Stress.* Carmarthen: Crown House Publishing.

Jacobson, Edmund (1938, repr. 1974). *Progressive Relaxation* (Midway Reprint). Chicago: University of Chicago Press.

Kabat-Zinn, J. (1990) *Full Catastrophe Living: Using the Wisdom of Your Body and Mind to Face Stress, Pain and Illness.* New York: Dell Publishing.

Kessler, R. C., Berglund, P., Demler, O., Jin, R., Merikangas, K. R., & Walters, E. E. (2005). Lifetime prevalence and age-of-onset distributions of DSM-IV disorders in the National Comorbidity Survey Replication. *Archives of General Psychiatry*, 62(6), 593–602.

Kessler, R. C., Chiu, W. T., Demler, O., & Walters, E. E. (2005). Prevalence, severity, and comorbidity of 12-month DSM-IV disorders in the National Comorbidity Survey Replication. *Archives of General Psychiatry*, 62(6), 617–27.

Kessler, R. C., Chiu, W. T., Jin, R., Ruscio, A. M., Shear, K., & Walters, E. E. (2006). The epidemiology of panic attacks, panic disorder, and agoraphobia in the National Comorbidity Survey Replication. *Archives of General Psychiatry*, 63(4), 415–24.

Kessler, R. C., Demler, O., Frank, R. G., Olfson, M., Pincus, H. A., Walters, E. E., Wang, P., Wells, K. B., & Zaslavsky, A. M. (2005). Prevalence and treatment of mental disorders 1990 to 2003. *New England Journal of Medicine*, 352(24), 2515–23.

Kessler, R. C., Sonnega, E., Bromet, M., & Hughes, C. B. (1995). Posttraumatic stress disorder in the National Comorbidity Survey. *Archives of General Psychiatry*, 52 (12),

Kessler, R. C., Stein, M. B., & Berglund, P. (1998). Social phobia subtypes in the National Comorbidity Survey. *American Journal of Psychiatry*, 155, 613–19.

Kushner, M. G., Sher, K. J., & Beitman, B. D. (1990). The relation between alcohol problems and the anxiety disorders. *American Journal of Psychiatry*, 147, 685–95.

Lambert, M. J. (1992). Psychotherapy outcome research: Implications for integrative and eclectic therapists, in J. C. Norcross, & M. R. Goldfried (eds.), *Handbook of Psychotherapy Integration* (pp. 94–129). New York: Basic Books.

Lecrubier, Y. (1998). Comorbidity in social anxiety disorder: impact on disease burden and management. *Journal of Clinical Psychiatry*, 59, 33–8.

Linehan, M. (1993). *Skills Training Manual for Treating Borderline Personality Disorder.* New York: Guilford Press.

Litz, B. T., Penk, W. E., Gerardi, R. J., & Keane, T. M. (1992). Assessment of post-traumatic stress disorder, in P. A. Saigh (ed.), *Posttraumatic Stress Disorder: A Behavioral Approach to Assessment and Treatment* (pp. 50–83). Boston, MA: Allyn & Bacon.

Lydiard, R. B. (2001). Social anxiety disorder treatment: the role of SSRIs, in S. A. Montgomery & J. A. den Boer (eds.), *Perspectives in Psychiatry, Vol. 8: SSRIs in Depression and Anxiety* (2nd ed.) (pp. 129–50). New York: John Wiley & Sons.

McIntosh, A., Cohen, A., Turnbull, N., Esmonde, L., Dennis, P., Eatock, J., Feetam, C., Hague, J., Hughes, I., Kelly, J., Kosky, N., Lear, G., Owens, L., Ratcliffe, J., & Salkovskis, P. (2004). *Clinical Guidelines and Evidence Review for Panic Disorder and Generalised Anxiety Disorder*. Sheffield: University of Sheffield/London: National Collaborating Centre for Primary Care.

Marks, I. M., & Mathews, A. M. (1979). Brief standard self-rating for phobic patients. *Behavior Research and Therapy*, 17, 263–7.

Marks, I. M., Stern, R. S., Mawson, D., Cobb, J., & McDonald, R. (1980). Clomipramine and exposure for obsessive–compulsive rituals. *British Journal of Psychiatry*, 136, 1–25.

Maslow, A. (1954). *Motivation and Personality*. New York: Harper.

Menzies, R. G., & de Silva, P. (eds.) (2003). *Obsessive–Compulsive Disorder: Theory, Research and Treatment*. Chichester: John Wiley.

Meyer, V. (1966). Modification of expectations in cases with obsessional rituals. *Behaviour Research and Therapy*, 4, 273–80.

Orlinsky, D. E., Grawe, K., & Park, B. K. (1994). Process and outcome in psychotherapy, in A. E. Bergin & S. L. Garfield (eds.), *Handbook of Psychotherapy and Behavior Change* (4th edn), (pp. 270–378). New York: Wiley.

Prochaska, J. O., & DiClemente, C. C. (1983). Stages and processes of self-change of smoking: toward an integrative model of change. *Journal of Consulting and Clinical Psychology*, 51(3), 390–5.

Prochaska, J. O., & Norcross, J. C. (2001). Stages of change. *Psychotherapy*, 38 (4), 443–8.

Rickard, H. C., Scogin, F., & Keith, S. (1994). A one year follow-up of relaxation training for elders with subjective anxiety. *Gerontologist*, 34, 121–2.

Robins, L. N., & Regier, D. A. (1991). *Psychiatric Disorders in America*. New York: Free Press.

Salkovskis, P. M. (1989). Cognitive-behavioural factors and the persistence of intrusive thoughts in obsessive problems. *Behaviour Research and Therapy*, 23, 571–83.

Sanderson, W. C., DiNardo, P. A., Rapee, R. M., & Barlow, D. H. (1990). Syndrome comorbidity in patients diagnosed with DSM-III-R anxiety disorder. *Journal of Abnormal Psychology*, 99, 308–12.

Sareen, J., Cox, B. J., Afifi, T. O., de Graaf, R., Asmundson, G. J. G., ten Have, M., & Stein, M. B. (2005). Anxiety disorders and risk for suicidal ideation and suicidal attempts: a population-based longitudinal study for adults. *Archives of General Psychiatry*, 62(11), 1249–57.

Schneier, F. R., Johnson, J., Hornig, C. D., Liebowitz, M. R., & Weissman, M. M. (1992). Social phobia: comorbidity and morbidity in an epidemiological sample. *Archives of General Psychiatry*, 49, 282–8.

Scogin, F., Rickard, H. C., Keith, S., & Wilson, J. (1992). Progressive and imaginal relaxation training for elderly persons with subjective anxiety. *Psychology & Aging*, 7, 419–24.

Segal, Z. V., Williams, M. G., & Teasdale, J. D. (2002) *Mindfulness-based Cognitive Therapy for Depression: A New Approach to Preventing Relapse*. New York: Guilford Press.

Singleton, N., Bumpstead, R., O'Brien, M., Lee, A., & Meltzer, H. (2001). *Psychiatric Morbidity Among Adults Living in Private Households*. London: TSO.

Skinner, B. F. (1938) *The Behaviour of Organisms*. New York: Appleton-Century-Crofts.

Skinner, B. F. (1953) *Science and Human Behaviour*. New York: Macmillan.

Stanley, M. A., & Turner, S. M. (1995). Current status of pharmacological and behavioural treatment of obsessive–compulsive disorder. *Behaviour Therapy*, 26,163–86.

Stein, D. J., Spandaccini, E., & Hollander, E. (1995). Meta-analysis of pharmacotherapy trials for obsessive–compulsive disorder. *International Clinical Psychopharmacology*, 10, 11–18.

Steketee, G. S. (1993). *Treatment of Obsessive Compulsive Disorder*. New York: Guilford Press.

Van Ameringen, M., Mancini, C., Styan, G., & Donison, D. (1991). Relationship of social phobia with other psychiatric illness. *Journal of Affective Disorders*, 21, 93–9.

van Oppen, P., & Arntz, A. (1994). Cognitive therapy for obsessive–compulsive disorder. *Behaviour Research and Therapy*, 31(1), 79–87.

Watson, J. B. (1913) Psychology as the behaviorist views it. *Psychological Review*, 20, 158–77

Wells, A. (1997). *Cognitive Therapy of Anxiety Disorders: A Practice Manual and Conceptual Guide*. New York: Wiley.

Wilson, R. R. (2003). *Facing Panic: Self-help for People with Panic Attacks*, Silver Spring, MD: ADAA.

Yerkes, R. M., & Dodson, J. D. (1908). The relation of strength of stimulus to rapidity of habit-formation. *Journal of Comparative Neurology and Psychology*, 18, 459–82.

Index

Also Available

Relaxation Techniques

Reduce Stress and Anxiety and Enhance Well-Being

Lillian Nejad PhD and
Katerina Volny BSc

Stressed?

Learn techniques that will change your life.

On this CD you will find relaxation exercises that have been shown to be effective in reducing and managing the symptoms of stress and anxiety.

To make learning simple clear instructions are provided before each exercise. Use the seven simple, yet powerful, techniques to experience relaxation every day. By repeated practice of the relaxation exercises you can overcome stress and anxiety for a more healthful, improved lifestyle.

This CD can be used independently or in conjunction with *Treating Stress and Anxiety: A Practitioner's Guide to Evidence-Based Approaches* or other psychotherapy approaches.

ISBN: 978-184590078-6

Tracks include:

1. Introduction to Relaxation 2.14
2. Guidelines to Relaxation 2.10
3. Abdominal Breathing: Introduction 0.36
4. Abdominal Breathing: Exercise 7.32
5. Progressive Muscle Relaxation: Introduction 0.48
6. Progressive Muscle Relaxation: Exercise 18.39
7. Visualization: Introduction 1.53
8. Beach Visualization 5.48
9. Forest Visualization 6.41
10. Coping Induction: Introduction 0.59
11. Coping Induction: Exercise 11.40
12. Walking Relaxation: Introduction 1.30
13. Walking Relaxation: Exercise 5.42
14. Brief Relaxation: Introduction 0.37
15. Brief Relaxation: Exercise 2.54

www.crownhouse.co.uk – www.chpus.com